Carpenters and Builders Library Volume Four

Millwork, Power Tools, Painting

by John E. Ball

Revised and Edited by Tom Philbin

★★★★

Theodore Audel & Co.
A Division of
The Bobbs-Merrill Co., Inc.
Indianapolis/New York

FIFTH EDITION
FIRST PRINTING—1982

Library of Congress Cataloging in Publication Data

Ball, John E.
  Millwork, power tools, painting.

    (Carpenters and builders library/by John E. Ball ; v. 4)
    Includes index.
    1. Millwork (Woodwork) 2. Power tools.
3. House painting. I. Philbin, Tom, 1934-
II. Title. III. Series: Ball, John E.
Carpenters and builders library ; v. 4.
TS878.B34 1982 694   82-1332
ISBN 0-672-23368-1   AACR2
Published by The Bobbs-Merrill Company, Inc.
Indianapolis/New York

Foreword

This volume, the fourth in a complete library for carpenters, do-it-yourselfers, and builders, covers a wide range of areas, many of them in the "finishing touch" category.

Chapter 1, for example, discusses roofing, from the latest roof types to how to install a number of roofs, including asphalt shingle roofs, which are far and away the most popular.

There is also a chapter on what is available in doors and windows. These are two very important areas today; both can play a role in energy saving.

Such details as cornice construction and working with moldings, which often get lost in the shuffle, are also included here, as is protecting the home against termites.

For plain good looks, there is an examination of what is available in flooring, and for walls and ceilings. And there is an in-depth discussion about paints and painting.

A large portion of the book should appeal to those who value good tools. There is a comprehensive section on tools plus step-by-step instructions on using a wide variety of power tools. There are stationary tools—table saw, bench saw, drill press, shaper, planer, and others—and portable tools—circular saw, saber saw, electric drill—all the machinery that makes projects go faster and better.

Finally, so that nobody will be at a loss for words, there is a glossary of housing terms.

Good luck.

Contents

woodturning operations—polishing—summary—review
questions

spray painting—care of equipment—summary—review
questions

CHAPTER 1

Roofing

A roof includes the roof cover (the upper layer that protects against rain, snow, and wind), the sheathing to which it is fastened, and the framing (rafters) that supports the whole structure.

The term roofing, or roof cover, refers to the uppermost part of a roof. Because of its exposure, roofing usually has a relatively limited life, and so is made to be readily replaceable. It may be made of many different materials, among which are the following:

1. Wood, usually in the form of shingles (uniform, machine cut) or shakes (hand cut). See Fig. 1.
2. Metal or aluminum, which simulates other kinds of roofing.
3. Slate, which may be the natural product, or rigid manufactured slabs, often of cement-asbestos.
4. Tile, which is a burned clay or shale product. Several standard types are available.
5. Built-up covers of asphalt- or tar-impregnated felts, with moppings of hot tar or asphalt between the plies and a mopping of tar or asphalt over all. With tar-felt roofs, the top is usually covered with embedded gravel or crushed slag.
6. Roll roofing, which, as the name implies, is marketed in rolls containing approximately 108 square feet. Each roll is usually 36 inches wide and may be plain or have a coating of various colored mineral granules. The base is a heavy asphalt-impregnated felt.

Fig. 1. Wood shakes handsomely top this lovely home. Wood shingles, which give a more uniform appearance, are also available. Courtesy of Scholz Homes.

7. Asphalt shingles, usually in the form of strips with two, three, or four tabs per unit. These shingles are asphalt, with the surface exposed to the weather heavily coated with mineral granules. Because of their fire-resistance, cost, and reasonably good durability, this is the most popular roofing material for residences (Fig. 2). Asphalt shingles are available in a wide range of colors, including black and white.

8. Glass fiber shingles, which are made partly of a glass fiber mat that is waterproof and partly of asphalt. Like asphalt shingles, glass fiber shingles come with self-sealing tabs and carry a Class A fire-resistance warranty (Fig. 3). For the do-it-yourselfer they may be of special interest because they are lightweight, about 220 pounds per square (Fig. 4).

SLOPE OF ROOFS

The slope of the roof is frequently a factor in the choice of roofing materials and in the method used to put them in place.

Fig. 2. Asphalt shingles being installed on a wood shingle roof. Asphalt is now the most popular roofing.

The lower the pitch of the roof, the greater is the chance of wind getting under the shingles and tearing them out. Interlocking cedar shingles resist this wind prying better than the standard asphalt shingles. For roofs with less than a 4-inch slope per foot, do not use standard asphalt. Down to 2 inches, use self-sealing. Roll roofing can be used with pitches down to 2 inches when lapped 2 inches. For very low-pitched slopes, the manufacturers of asphalt shingles recommend that the roof be planned for some other type of covering.

Aluminum strip roofing virutally eliminates the problem of wind prying, but it is noisy. Most homeowners object to the noise during a rainstorm. Even on porches, this noise is often annoying inside the house.

Spaced roofing boards are sometimes used with cedar shingles as an economy measure and because the cedar shingles themselves add considerably to the strength of the roof. The spaced roofing boards reduce the insulating qualities, however, and it is advisable to use a tightly sheathed roof beneath the shingles if the need for insulation overcomes the need for economy.

Fig. 3. Glass fiber shingles are light in weight and have a high fire-resistance rating. Courtesy of Owens-Corning.

For drainage, most roofs should have a certain amount of slope. Roofs covered with tar-and-gravel coverings are theoretically satisfactory when built level, but standing water may ultimately do harm. If you can avoid a flat roof, do so. Level roofs drain very slowly, and slightly smaller eave troughs and downspouts are used on these roofs. They are quite common on industrial and commercial buildings.

ROLL ROOFING

Roll roofing (Fig. 5) is an economical cover especially suited for roofs with low pitches; it also is sometimes used for valley flashing instead of metal. Roll roofing has a base of heavy

Fig. 4. These shingles look like slate, but they are actually glass fiber.
Courtesy of Owens-Corning.

asphalt-impregnated felt with additional coatings of asphalt that are dusted to prevent adhesion in the roll. The weather surface may be plain or covered with fine mineral granules. Many different colors are available. One edge of the sheet is left plain (no granules) where the lap cement is applied. For best results, the sheathing must be tight, preferably 1 × 6 tongue-and-groove, or plywood. If the sheathing is smooth, with no cupped boards or other protuberance, the slate-surfaced roll roofings will withstand a surprising amount of abrasion from foot traffic, although it is not generally recommended for that purpose. Windstorms are the most relentless enemy of roll roofings. If the wind gets under a loose edge, almost certainly a section will be blown off.

BUILT-UP ROOF

A built-up roof is constructed of sheathing paper, a bonded base sheet, perforated felt, asphalt, and surface aggregates (Fig. 6). The sheathing paper comes in 36-inch-wide rolls and has approximately 500 square feet per roll. It is a rosin-size paper and is used to prevent asphalt leakage to the wood deck. The base

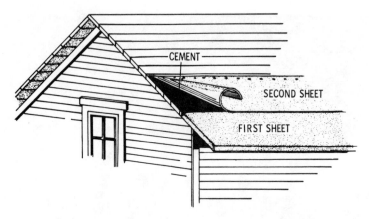

Fig. 5. First and second strips of roll roofing installed.

sheet is a heavy asphalt saturated felt that is placed over the sheathing paper. It is available in 1-, 1½-, and 2-inch-square rolls. The perforated felt is one of the primary parts of a built-up roof. It is saturated with asphalt and has tiny perforations throughout the sheet. The perforations prevent air entrapment between the layers of felt. The perforated felt is 36 inches wide and weighs approximately 15 pounds per square. Asphalt is also one of the basic ingredients of a built-up roof. There are many different grades of asphalt, but the most common are low melt, medium melt, high melt, and extra high melt.

Prior to the application of the built-up roof, the deck should be inspected for soundness. Wood board decks should be con-

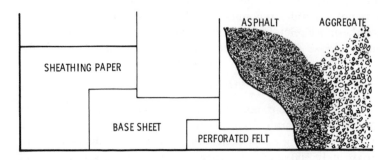

Fig. 6. Sectional plan of a built-up roof.

structed of $3/4$-inch seasoned lumber. Any knotholes larger than 1 inch should be covered with sheet metal. If plywood is used as a roof deck, it should be placed at right angles to the rafters and be at least $1/2$ inch in thickness.

The first step in the application of a built-up roof is the placing of sheathing paper and base sheet. The sheathing paper should be lapped 2 inches and secured with just enough nails to hold it in place. The base sheet is then placed with 2-inch side laps and 6-inch end laps. The base sheet should be secured with $1/2$-inch-diameter head galvanized roofing nails placed 12 inches on center on the exposed lap. Nails should also be placed down the center of the base sheet. The nails should be placed in two parallel rows 12 inches apart.

The base sheet is then coated with a uniform layer of hot asphalt. While the asphalt is still hot, layers of roofing felt are placed. Each sheet is then coated with a uniform layer of hot asphalt. While the asphalt is still hot, layers of roofing felt are placed. Each sheet should be lapped 19 inches, leaving an exposed lap of 17 inches.

Once the roofing felt is placed, a gravel stop is installed around the deck perimeter (Fig. 7). Two coated layers of felt should extend 6 inches past the roof decking where the gravel stop is to be installed. When the other plies are placed, the first two layers are folded over the other layers and mopped in place. The gravel stop is then placed in a $1/8$-inch-thick bed of flashing cement and securely nailed every 6 inches. The ends of the gravel stop should be lapped 6 inches and packed in flashing cement.

After the gravel stop is placed, the roof is flooded with hot asphalt and the surface aggregate is embedded in the flood coat. The aggregates should be hard, dry, opaque, and free of any dust or foreign matter. The size of the aggregates should range from $1/4$ inch to $5/8$ inch. When the aggregate is piled on the roof, it should be placed on a spot that has been mopped with asphalt. This technique assures proper adhesion in all areas of the roof.

WOOD SHINGLES

The better grades of wood shingles are made of cypress, cedar, and redwood and are available in lengths of 16 and 18 inches and thicknesses at the butt of $^5/_{16}$ inch and $^7/_{16}$ inch, respectively. They are packaged in bundles of approximately 200 shingles in random width from 3 to 12 inches.

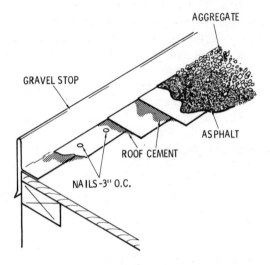

Fig. 7. Illustrating the gravel stop.

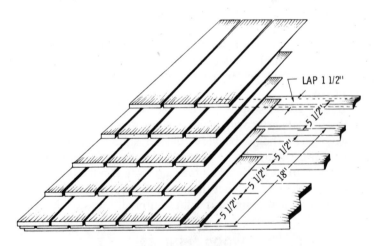

Fig. 8. Section of a shingle roof illustrating the amount of shingle which may be exposed to the weather as governed by the lap.

An important requirement in applying wood shingles is that each shingle should lap over the two courses below it, so that there will always be at least three layers of shingles at every point on the roof. This requires that the amount of shingle exposed to the weather (the spacing of the courses) should be less than one-third the length of the shingle. Thus in Fig. 8, $5^1/_2$ inches is the maximum amount that 18-inch shingles can be laid to the weather and have an adequate amount of lap. This is further shown in Fig. 9A.

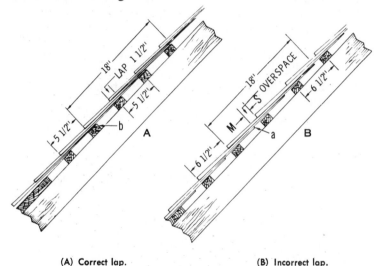

(A) Correct lap.   (B) Incorrect lap.

Fig. 9. The amount of lap is an important factor in applying wood shingles.

In case the shingles are laid more than one-third of their length to the weather, there will be a space, as shown by MS in Fig. 9B, where only two layers of shingles will cover the roof. This is objectionable, because if the top shingle splits above the edge of the shingle below, water will leak through. The maximum spacing to the weather for 16-inch shingles should be $4\frac{7}{8}$ inches, and for 18-inch shingles should be $5^1/_2$ inches. Strictly speaking, the amount of lap should be governed by the pitch of the roof. The maximum spacing may be followed for roofs of moderate pitch, but for roofs of small pitch, more lap should be allowed, and for a steep pitch the lap may be reduced somewhat, but it is not

17

advisable to do so. Wood shingles should not be used on pitches less than 4 inches per foot.

Table 1 shows the number of square feet that 1,000 (five bundles) shingles will cover for various exposures. This table does not allow for waste on hip and valley roofs.

Table 1. Space Covered by 1,000 Shingles

Exposure to weather	4¼	4½	4¾	5	5½	6
Area covered in sq. ft.	118	125	131	138	152	166

Shingles should not be laid too close together, for they will swell when wet, causing them to bulge and split. Seasoned shingles should not be laid with their edges nearer than $3/16$ inches when laid. It is advisable to soak the bundles thoroughly before opening.

Great care must be used in nailing wide shingles. When they are over 8 inches in width, they should be split and laid as two shingles. The nails should be spaced such that the space between them is as small as is practical, thus directing the contraction and expansion of the shingle toward the edges. This lessens the danger of wide shingles splitting in or near the center and over joints beneath. Shingling is always started from the bottom and laid from the eaves or cornice up.

There are various methods of laying shingles, the most common known as:

1. The straightedge.
2. The chalk-line.
3. The gauge-and-hatchet.

The straightedge method is one of the oldest. A straightedge having a width equal to the spacing to the weather or the distance between courses is used. This eliminates measuring, it being necessary only to keep the lower edge flush with the lower edge of the course of shingles just laid; the upper edge of the straightedge is then in line for the next course. This is considered to be the slowest of the three methods.

The chalk-line method consists in snapping a chalk line for each course. To save time, two or three lines may be snapped at the same time, making it possible to carry two or three courses at once. It is faster than the straightedge method, but not as fast as the gauge-and-hatchet method.

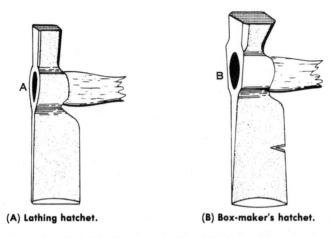

(A) Lathing hatchet.   (B) Box-maker's hatchet.

Fig. 10. Hatchets used in shingling.

The gauge-and-hatchet method is extensively used in western states. The hatchet used is either a lathing or a box-maker's hatchet, as shown in Fig. 10. Hatchet gauges to measure the space between courses are shown in Fig. 11. The gauge is set on the blade at a distance from the hatchet poll equal to the exposure desired for the shingles.

Nail as close to the butts as possible, if the nails will be well covered by the next course. Only galvanized shingle nails should be used. The 3d shingle nail is slightly larger in diameter than the 3d common nail, and has a slightly larger head.

Hips

The hip is less likely to leak than any other part of the roof as the water runs away from it. However, since it is so prominent, the work should be well done. Fig. 12 shows the method of cutting shingle butts for a hip roof. After the courses 1 and 2 are laid, the top corners over the hip are trimmed off with a sharp shingling hatchet kept keen for that purpose and shingle 3 with the butt cut so as to continue the straight line of courses and

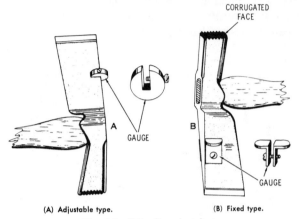

CORRUGATED
FACE

A

GAUGE

B

GAUGE

(A) Adjustable type.   (B) Fixed type.

Fig. 11. Shingling hatchet.

again on the dotted line 4, so that shingle *a*, of the second course, squares against it and so on from side to side, each alternately lapping the other at the hip joint. When gables are shingled, this same method may be used up the rake of the roof if the pitch is moderate to steep. It cannot be effectively used with flat pitches. The shingles used should be ripped to uniform width.

For best construction, metal shingles should be laid under the hip shingles, as shown in Fig. 13. These metal shingles should correspond in shape to that of hip shingles. They should be at least 7 inches wide and large enough to reach well under the metal shingles of the course above, as at *w*. At *a*, the metal shingles are laid so that the lower end will just be covered by the hip shingle of the course above.

Valleys

In shingling a valley, first a strip of aluminum or roll roofing, ordinarily 20 inches wide, is laid in the valley. Fig. 14 illustrates an open-type valley. Here the dotted lines show the aluminum or other material used as flashing under the shingles. If the pitch is above 30°, then a width of 16 inches is sufficient; if flatter, the width should be more. In a long valley, its width between shingles should increase in width from top to bottom about 1 inch,

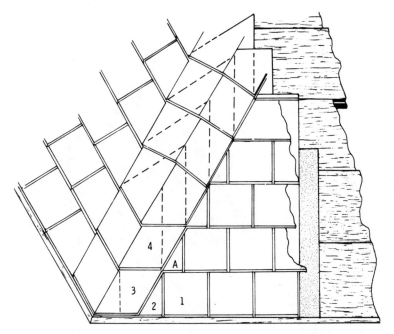

Fig. 12. Hip roof shingling.

Fig. 13. Method of installing
metal shingles under
wooden shingles.

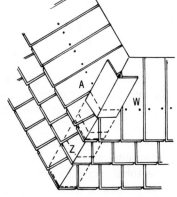

and at the top 2 inches is ample width. This is to prevent ice or other objects from wedging when slipping down. The shingles taper to the butt, the reverse of the hip, and need no reinforcing, as the thin edge is held and protected from splitting off by the

21

shingle above it. Care must always be taken to nail the shingle nearest the valley as far from it as practical by placing the nail higher up.

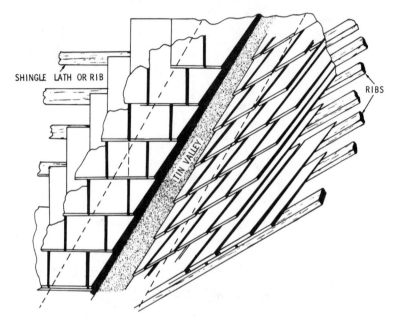

Fig. 14. Method of shingling a valley.

ASPHALT SHINGLES

Asphalt shingles are made in strips of two, three, or four units or tabs joined together, as well as in the form of individual shingles. When laid, strip shingles furnish practically the same pattern as undivided shingles. Both strip and individual types are available in different shapes, sizes, and colors to suit various requirements.

Asphalt shingles must be applied on slopes having an incline of 4 inches or more to the foot. Before the shingles are laid, the underlayment should be placed. The underlayment should be 15-lb. asphalt-saturated felt. This material should be placed with 2-inch side laps and 4-inch end laps (Fig. 15). The underlayment serves three purposes: (1) it acts as a primary barrier against

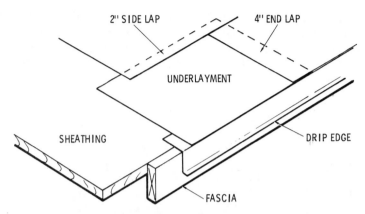

Fig. 15. Application of the underlayment.

moisture penetration, (2) it acts as a secondary barrier against moisture penetration, and (3) it acts as a buffer between the resinous areas of the decking and the asphalt shingles. A heavy felt should not be used as underlayment. The heavy felt would act as a vapor barrier and would permit the accumulation of moisture between the underlayment and the roof deck.

The roof deck may be constructed of well seasoned 1″ × 6″ tongue-and-groove sheathing or plywood. The boards should be secured with two 8d nails in each rafter. Plywood should be placed with the long dimension perpendicular to the rafters. The plywood should never be less than ⅜ inch thick.

To efficiently shed water at the roof's edge, a drip edge is usually installed. A drip edge is constructed of corrosion-resistant sheet metal and extends 3 inches back from the roof edge. To form the drip-edge the sheet metal is bent down over the roof edges.

The nails used to apply asphalt shingles should be hot-galvanized nails with large heads, sharp points, and barbed shanks. The nails should be long enough to penetrate the roof decking at least ¾ inch.

To ensure proper shingle alignment, horizontal and vertical chalk lines should be snapped on the underlayment. It is usually recommended that the lines be placed 10 or 20 inches apart. The first course of shingles placed is the starter course; this is used to back up the first regular course of shingles and to fill in the spaces between the tabs. It is placed with the tabs facing up the roof and is allowed to project 1 inch over the rake and eave (Fig. 16). To ensure that all cutouts are covered 3 inches should be cut off the first starter shingle.

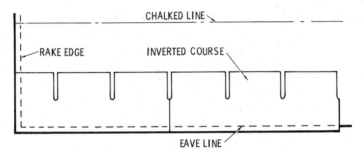

CHALKED LINE

RAKE EDGE INVERTED COURSE

EAVE LINE

Fig. 16. The starter course.

Once the starter course has been placed, the different courses of shingles can be laid. The first regular course of shingles should be started with a full shingle; the second course with a full shingle, minus one-half a tab; the third course is started with a full shingle (Fig. 17); and the process is repeated. As the shingles are placed, they should be properly nailed (Fig. 18). If a three-tab shingle is used, a minimum of 4 nails per strip should be used. The nails should be placed 5⅝ inches from the bottom of the shingle and should be located over the cutouts. The nails on each end of the shingle should be located one inch from the end. The nails should be driven straight and flush with the surface of the shingle.

If there is a valley in the roof, it must be properly flashed. The two materials that are most often used for valley flashing are 90-lb. mineral-surfaced asphalt roll roofing or galvanized sheet metal. The flashing is 18 inches in width and should extend the full length of the valley. Before the shingles are laid to the valley chalked lines are placed along the valley. The chalk lines should be 6 inches apart at the top of the valley and should widen ⅛ inch per foot as they approach the eave line. The shingles are laid up to the chalked lines and trimmed to fit.

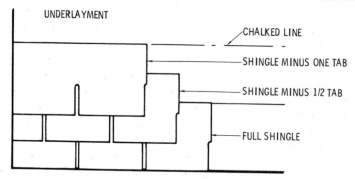

UNDERLAYMENT

CHALKED LINE

SHINGLE MINUS ONE TAB

SHINGLE MINUS 1/2 TAB

FULL SHINGLE

Fig. 17. Application of the starter shingles.

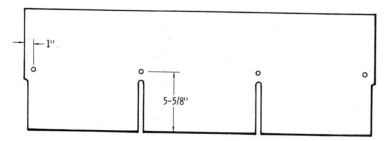

1"

5-5/8"

Fig. 18. The proper placement of nails.

Hips and ridges are finished by using manufactured hip and ridge units, or hip and ridge units cut from a strip shingle. If the unit is cut from a strip shingle, the two cut lines should be cut at an angle (Fig. 19). This will prevent the projection of the shingle past the overlaid shingle. Each shingle should be bent down the center so that there is an equal distance on each side. In cold weather the shingles should be warmed before they are bent. Starting at the bottom of the hip or at the end of a ridge, the shingles are placed with a 5-inch exposure. To secure the shingles, a nail is placed on each side of the shingle. The nails should be placed 5½ inches back from the exposed edge and 1 inch up from the side.

If the roof slope is particularly steep, specifically if it exceeds 60° or 21 inches per foot, then special procedures are required for securing the shingles. This is shown in Fig. 20.

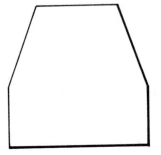

Fig. 19. Hips shingles.

Two other details. For neatness when installing asphalt shingles, the courses should meet in a line above any dormer (Fig. 21). And, of course, ventilation must be provided for an asphalt, or really, for any kind of roof, as indicated in Fig. 22.

SLATE

Slate is not used as much as it once was, but it is still used. The process of manufacture is to split the quarried slate blocks horizontally to a suitable thickness, and to cut vertically to the approximate sizes required. The slates are then passed through planers, and after the operation are ready to be reduced to the exact dimensions on rubbing beds or through the use of air tools and other special machinery.

Roofing slate is usually available in various colors and in standard sizes suitable for the most exacting requirements. On all boarding to be covered with slate, asphalt-saturated rag felt of certain specified thickness is required. This felt should be laid in a horizontal layer with joints lapped toward the eaves and at the ends at least 2 inches. A well-secured lap at the end is necessary to properly hold the felt in place, and to protect the structure until covered by the slate. In laying the slate, the entire surface of all main and porch roofs should be covered with slate in a proper and watertight manner.

The slate should project 2 inches at the eaves and 1 inch at all gable ends, and should be laid in horizontal courses with the standard 3-inch headlap. Each course should break joints with the preceding one. Slates at the eaves or cornice line should be doubled and canted ¼ inch by a wooden cant strip. Slates over-

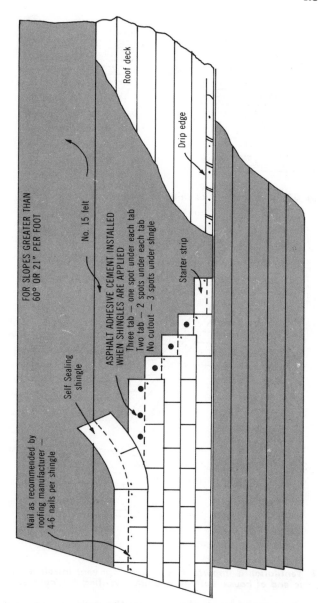

Fig. 20. When a roof has a severe slope, special installation procedures are required for asphalt shingles.

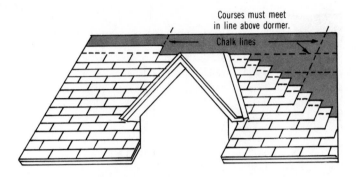

Fig. 21. Arrangement of shingles when there is a dormer.

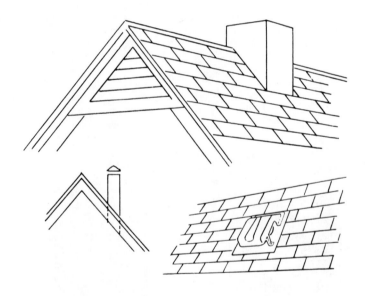

Fig. 22. Ventilation is important in roofing. Top: vent installed high on gable end of house. Bottom: two other venting arrangements.

lapping sheet-metal work should have the nails so placed as to avoid puncturing the sheet metal. Exposed nails should be used only in courses where unavoidable. Neatly fit the slate around any pipes, ventilators, etc.

Nails should not be driven in so far as to produce a strain on the slate. Cover all exposed nail heads with elastic cement. Hip slates and ridge slates should be laid in elastic cement spread thickly over unexposed surfaces. Build in and place all flashing pieces furnished by the sheeting contractor and cooperate with him in doing the work of flashing. On completion, all slate must be sound, whole, and clean, and the roof should be left in every respect tight and a neat example of workmanship.

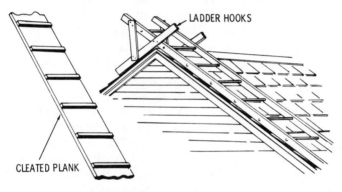

Fig. 23. Illustrating two types of supports used in repairs of roof.

The most frequently needed repair of slate roofs is the replacement of broken slates. When such replacements are necessary, supports similar to those shown in Fig. 23 should be placed on the roof to distribute the weight of the roofers while they are working. Broken slates should be removed by cutting or drawing out the nails with a ripper tool. A new slate shingle of the same color and size as the old should be inserted and fastened by nailing through the vertical joint of the slates in the overlying course approximately 2 inches below the butt of the slate in the second course, as shown in Fig. 24.

A piece of sheet copper or terneplate about 3″ × 8″ should be inserted over the nail head to extend about 2 inches under the second course above the replaced shingle. The metal strip should be bent slightly before being inserted so that it will stay

29

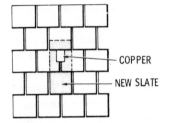

COPPER

NEW SLATE

Fig. 24. Method of inserting new pieces of slate shingles.

securely in place. Very old slate roofs sometimes fail because the nails used to fasten the slates have rusted. In such cases, the entire roof covering should be removed and replaced, including the felt underlay materials. The sheathing and rafters should be examined and any broken boards replaced with new material. All loose boards should be nailed in place, and before laying the felt, the sheathing should be swept clean, protruding nails driven in, and any rough edges trimmed smooth.

If the former roof was slate, all slates that are still in good condition may be salvaged and relaid. New slates should be the same size as the old ones and should match the original slates as nearly as possible in color and texture. The area to be covered should govern the size of slates to be used and whatever the size, the slates may be of random widths, but they should be of uniform length and punched for a head lap of not less than 3 inches. The roof slates should be laid with a 3-inch head lap and fastened with two large-head slating nails. Nails should not be driven too tight, the nail heads barely touch the slate. All slates within 1 foot of the top and along the gable rakes of the roof should be bedded in flashing cement.

GUTTERS AND DOWNSPOUTS

Most roofs require gutters and downspouts in order to carry the water away from the foundation. They are usually made of aluminum, steel, wood, or plastic. In regions of heavy snowfall, the outer edge of the gutter should be ½ inch below the extended slope of the roof to prevent snow banking on the edge of the roof and causing leaks. The hanging gutter is best adapted to such construction.

Downspouts should be large enough to remove the water from

the gutters. A common fault is to make the gutter outlet the same size as the downspout. At 18 inches below the gutter, a downspout has nearly four times the water-carrying capacity of the inlet at the gutter. Therefore, a good-sized ending to the downspout should be provided. Wire baskets or guards should be placed at gutter outlets to prevent leaves and trash from collecting in the downspouts and causing damage during freezing weather.

The most popular kind of gutter is made of aluminum. It comes in two common gauges, .027 and .032, with the thicker material better, of course. Standard lengths are 10 feet, and they are joined by special connectors (Fig. 25) using either sheet metal screws or blind rivets—blind rivets are simplest.

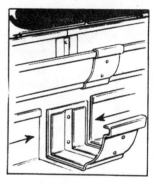

Fig. 25. A gutter section connector.

Any connection, however, represents an area that can leak. It is better to get so-called seamless gutter. Fabricators will custom-cut it to fit on your side to any length. You will also save installation time. Seamless gutter is commonly .032 gauge.

Fittings for gutters vary from manufacturer to manufacturer (Figs. 26 and 27). At any rate, they are not difficult to install, as the illustrations indicate.

One caution vis-à-vis gutters. They should have the proper slope for good runoff of water—about ½ inch to every 10 feet. Some people make the mistake of sloping one gutter according to the way the house appears. But this can lead to errors because a house, although it may look level, never really is, and to use the house as a guide for gutter placement is hazardous (Fig. 28).

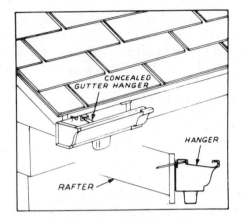

Fig. 26. Gutter can be hung with concealed hangers.

Fig. 27. Spikes and ferrules are a popular way of installing a metal gutter.

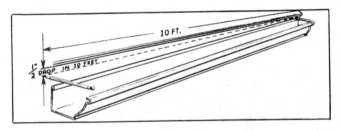

Fig. 28. Gutter should slope ½ inch per 10 feet.

SELECTING ROOFING MATERIALS

Roofing materials are commonly sold by dealers or manufacturers on the basis of quantities sufficient to cover 100 square feet. This quantity is commonly termed "one square" by roofers and in trade literature. When ordering roofing material, it will be well to make allowance for waste, such as in hips, valleys, and starter courses. This applies in general to all types of roofing.

The slope of the roof and the strength of the framing are the first determining factors in choosing a suitable covering. If the slope is slight, there will be danger of leaks with a wrong kind of covering, and excessive weight may cause sagging that is unsightly and adds to the difficulty of keeping the roof in repair. The cost of roofing depends to a great extent on the type of roof to be covered. A roof having ridges, valleys, dormers, or chimneys will cost considerably more to cover than one having a plain surface. Very steep roofs are also more expensive than those with a flatter slope, but most roofing materials last longer on steep grades than on low-pitched roofs. Frequently, nearness to supply centers permits the use, at lower cost, of the more durable materials instead of the commonly lower-priced, shorter-lived ones.

In considering cost, one should keep in mind maintenance and repair and the length of service expected from the building. A permanent structure warrants a good roof, even though the first cost is somewhat high. When the cost of applying the covering is high in comparison with the cost of the material, or when access to the roof is hazardous, the use of long-lived material is warranted. Unless insulation is required, semipermanent buildings and sheds are often covered with low-grade roofing.

Frequently, the importance of fire resistance is not recognized, and sometimes it is wrongly stressed. It is essential to have a covering that will not readily ignite from glowing embers. The building regulations of many cities prohibit the use of certain types of roofings in congested areas where fires may spread rapidly. The Underwriters Laboratories has grouped many different kinds and brands of roofing in classes from A to C according to the protection afforded against spread of fire. Class A is the best.

The appearance of a building can be changed materially by using the various coverings in different ways. Wood shingles and slate are often used to produce architectural effects. The roofs of buildings in a farm group should harmonize in color, even though similarity in contour is not always feasible.

All coal-tar pitch roofs should be covered with a mineral coating because when fully exposed to the sun, they deteriorate. Observation has shown that, in general, roofings with light-colored surfaces absorb less heat than those with dark surfaces. Considerable attention should be given to the comfort derived from a properly insulated roof. A thin uninsulated roof gives the interior little protection from heat in summer and cold in winter. Discomfort from summer heat can be lessened to some extent by ventilating the space under the roof. None of the usual roof coverings have any appreciable insulating value. If it is necessary to re-roof, consideration should be given to the feasibility of installing extra insulation under the roofing.

DETECTION OF ROOF LEAKS

A well-constructed roof should be properly maintained. Periodic inspections should be made to detect breaks, missing shingles, choked gutters, damaged flashings, and also defective mortar joints of chimneys, parapets, coping, and such. At the first appearance of damp spots on the ceilings or walls, a careful examination of the roof should be made to determine the cause, and the defect should be repaired promptly. When repairs are delayed, small defects extend rapidly and involve not only the roof covering but also the sheathing, framing, and interior.

Many of these defects can be readily repaired to keep water from the interior and extend the life of the roof. Large defects or failures should be repaired by men familiar with the work. On many types of roofs, an inexperienced man can do more damage than he can do good. Leaks are sometimes difficult to find, but an examination of the wet spots on a ceiling furnishes a clue to the probable location. In some cases, the actual leak may be some distance up the slope. If near a chimney or exterior wall, the leaks are probably caused by a defective or narrow flashing, loose mortar joints, or dislodged coping. On flat roofs, the trouble may be the result of clogged downspouts or an accumulation of water or snow on the roof higher than the flashing. Defective and loose flashing is not uncommon around scuttles, cupolas, and plumbing vent pipes. Roofing deteriorates more rapidly on a southern exposure than on a northern one, which is especially noticeable when wood or composition shingles are used.

Wet spots under plain roof areas are generally caused by holes in the covering. Frequently, the drip may occur much lower down the slope than the hole. Where attics are unsealed and roofing strips have been used, holes can be detected from the inside by light shining through. If a piece of wire is stuck through the hole, it can be located from the outside.

Sometimes gutters are so arranged that when choked, they overflow into the house, or ice accumulating on the eaves will form a ridge that backs up melting snow under the shingles. This is a common trouble if roofs are flat and the eaves wide. Leaky downspouts permit water to splash against the wall and the wind-driven water may find its way through a defect into the interior. The exact method to use in repairing depends on the kind of roofing and the nature and extent of the defect.

SUMMARY

The roof of a building includes the roof cover, which is protection against rain, snow, and wind; the sheathing, which is a base for the roof cover; and the rafters, which are the support for the entire roof structure.

The term "roofing" refers to the uppermost part of the roof. There are various types of roofing used, such as wood (which generally is in the form of shingles or shakes), aluminum, tile, roll roofing, asphalt and glass fiber.

Various types and styles of flashing are used when a roof connects to any vertical wall, such as chimneys, outside walls, etc. Flashing around chimneys and skylights is installed in the same general manner as for vertical walls. It is generally made from roll roofing material or sheet metal or aluminum bent to fit the contour of the vertical wall. It is essential for sealing joints.

Most roofs require rain gutters and downspouts in order to carry the water to the sewer or outlet. Gutters and downspouts are usually built of aluminum. Seamless .032 gutter is best. Downspouts should be large enough to remove the water from the gutters. Much gutter deterioration is caused by freezing water in low areas, rust, and restricted sections due to leaves or other debris.

REVIEW QUESTIONS

1. Name various types of roofing used.
2. What is flashing and why is it used?
3. Why can corrugated metal roofs be installed without roof sheathing?
4. How much coverage in square feet is "one square" of roofing?

CHAPTER 2

Cornice Construction

The cornice is that projection of the roof at the eaves that forms a connection between the roof and the side walls. The three general types of cornice construction are the *box*, the *closed*, and the *open*.

BOX CORNICES

The typical box cornice shown in Fig. 1 utilizes the rafter projection for nailing surfaces for the facia and soffit boards. The soffit provides a desirable area for inlet ventilators. A frieze board is often used at the wall to receive the siding. In climates where snow and ice dams may occur on overhanging eaves, the soffit of the cornice may be sloped outward and left open 1/4 inch at the facia board for drainage.

CLOSED CORNICES

The closed cornice shown in Fig. 2 has no rafter projection. The overhang consists only of a frieze board and a shingle or crown molding. This type is not so desirable as a cornice with a projection, because it gives less protection to the side walls.

WIDE BOX CORNICES

The wide box cornice in Fig. 3 requires forming members called lookouts, which serve as nailing surfaces and supports for the soffit board. The lookouts are nailed at the rafter ends and are also toenailed to the wall sheathing and directly to the studs.

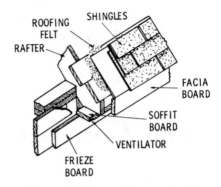

Fig. 1. Illustrating box cornice construction.

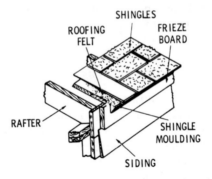

Fig. 2. Illustrating closed cornice construction.

The soffit can be of various materials, such as beaded ceiling, plywood, or bevel siding. A bed molding may be used at the juncture of the soffit and frieze. This type of cornice is often used in hip roof houses, and the facia board usually carries around the entire perimeter of the house.

OPEN CORNICES

The open cornice, shown in Fig. 4, may consist of a facia board nailed to the rafter ends. The frieze is either notched or cut out to fit between the rafters and is then nailed to the wall. The open cornice is often used for a garage. When it is used on a house, the roof boards are visible from below from the rafter ends to the wall line, and should consist of finished material. Dressed or matched V-beaded boards are often used.

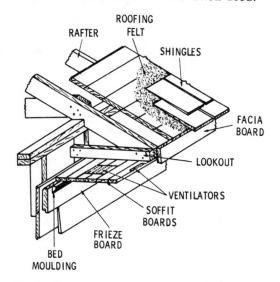

Fig. 3. Illustrating wide cornice construction.

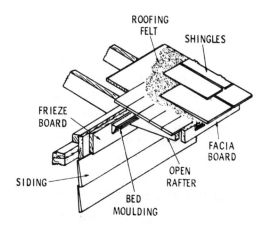

Fig. 4. Illustrating open cornice construction.

CORNICE RETURNS

The cornice return is the end finish of the cornice on a gable roof. The design of the cornice return depends to a large degree on the rake or gable projection, and on the type of cornice used. In a close rake (a gable end with very little projection), it is necessary to use a frieze or rake board as a finish for siding ends, as shown in Fig. 5. This board is usually $1\frac{1}{8}$ inches thick and follows the roof slope to meet the return of the cornice facia. Crown molding or other type of finish is used at the edge of the shingles.

CROWN
MOULDING

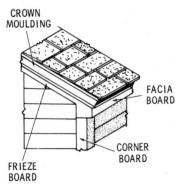

FACIA
BOARD

CORNER
BOARD

FRIEZE
BOARD

Fig. 5. Illustrating the closed cornice return.

When the gable end and the cornice have some projection, as shown in Fig. 6, a box return may be used. Trim on the rake projection is finished at the cornice return. A wide cornice with a small gable projection may be finished as shown in Fig. 7. Many variations of this trim detail are possible. For example, the frieze board at the gable end might be carried to the rake line and mitered with a facia board of the cornice. This siding is then carried across the cornice end to form a return.

RAKE OR GABLE-END FINISH

The rake section is that trim used along the gable end of a house. There are three general types commonly used; the *closed,* the *box with a projection,* and the *open.* The closed rake, as shown in Fig. 8, often consists of a frieze or a rake board with a crown molding as the finish. A $1'' \times 2''$ square edge molding is

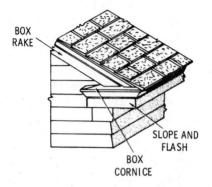

BOX
RAKE

SLOPE AND
FLASH

BOX
CORNICE

Fig. 6. Illustrating the box cornice return.

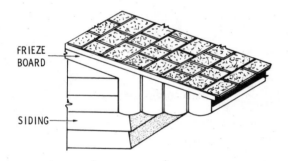

FRIEZE
BOARD

SIDING

Fig. 7. Illustrating the wide cornice return.

**Fig. 8. Illustrating the closed
end finish.**

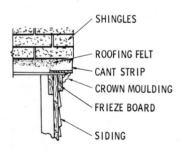

SHINGLES

ROOFING FELT

CANT STRIP

CROWN MOULDING

FRIEZE BOARD

SIDING

sometimes used instead of the crown molding. When fiber board sheathing is used, it is necessary to use a narrow frieze board that will leave a surface for nailing the siding into the end rafters.

41

If a wide frieze is used, nailing blocks must be provided between the studs. Wood sheathing does not require nailing blocks. The trim used for a box rake section requires the support of the projected roof boards, as shown in Fig. 9. In addition, lookouts or nailing blocks are fastened to the side wall and to the roof sheathing. These lookouts serve as a nailing surface for both the soffit and the facia boards. The ends of the roof boards are nailed to the facia. The frieze board is nailed to the side wall studs, and the crown and bed moldings complete the trim. The underside of the roof sheathing of the open projected rake, as shown in Fig. 10, is generally covered with liner boards such as $^5/_8$-inch beaded ceiling. The facia is held in place by nails through the roof sheathing.

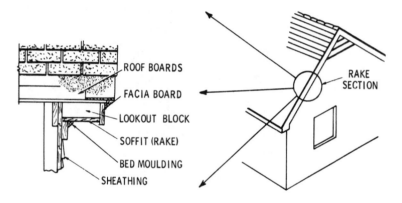

ROOF BOARDS
FACIA BOARD
LOOKOUT BLOCK
SOFFIT (RAKE)
BED MOULDING
SHEATHING

RAKE SECTION

Fig. 9. Illustrating the box end finish.

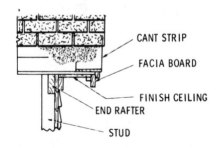

CANT STRIP
FACIA BOARD
FINISH CEILING
END RAFTER
STUD

Fig. 10. Illustrating the open end finish.

SUMMARY

The cornice is that part of the roof at the eaves that forms a connection between the roof and side walls. There are generally three styles of cornice construction, called box, closed, and open.

The box cornice construction generally uses the rafter ends as a nailing surface for the facia and soffit board. A board called the "frieze board" is used at the wall to start the wood siding. Wide box cornices require framework called lookouts, which serve as nailing surfaces and support the soffit board. The lookouts are nailed at the rafter end and also nailed at the other end to the wall stud.

On the closed cornice, there is no rafter projection. There is no overhang, using only a frieze board and molding. There is no protection from the weather for the side walls with this type of construction.

REVIEW QUESTIONS

1. Name the three types of cornice construction.
2. What is a frieze board?
3. Explain the purpose of the facia board.
4. What is the lookout block and when is it used?
5. What is the soffit board?

CHAPTER 3

Miter Work

By definition, a miter is the joint formed by two pieces of molding, each cut at an angle so as to match when joined angularly; also, to miter means to meet and match together on a line bisecting the angle of junction, especially at a right angle; in other words, to cut and join together the ends of two pieces obliquely at an angle.

MITER TOOLS

To do miter work with precision, the right tools are necessary. The first is, of course, the saw, which should be a good 20-inch backsaw of about eleven or twelve teeth to the inch, filed to a keen edge and rubbed off on the sides with the face of an oil stone. A serviceable miter box, such as the one shown in Fig. 1, can be made of suitable hardwood by the craftsman for most of the common miter cuts.

If you want an easier job of making miters, and increased precision, then consider purchasing one of the many metal miter boxes available (Fig. 2). These come with angle settings that lock in place, saw guides, and other features that very much simplify the job. Additionally you can obtain a motorized miter saw, as shown in Fig. 3. Here, all you do is lock the stock in place and cut across it.

MOLDINGS

In the ornamental side of carpentry construction, various forms of moldings, are, of course, used. Some of these are de-

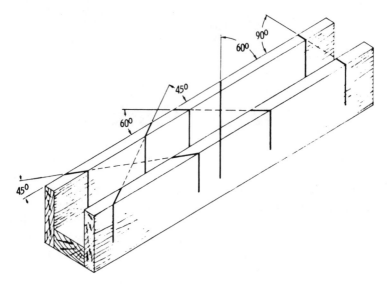

Fig. 1. Home-made miter box.

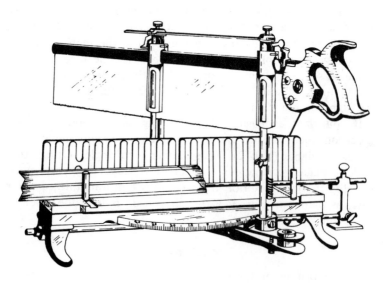

Fig. 2. A typical metal miter box with graduated scales of angle.

Fig. 3. Motorized miter saw. Courtesy of Sears, Roebuck & Co.

signed to lay flush or flat against the surfaces to which they are attached, as in Fig. 4; others are shaped to lie inclined at an angle to the nailing surfaces, as in Fig. 5. It is the *rake* or *spring* type molding that is hard to cut.

Mitering Flush Moldings

Where two pieces of molding join at right angles, as for instance the sides of a picture frame, the miter angle is 45°. The term "miter angle" means the angle formed by the miter cut and edge of the molding, as in Fig. 6.

In paneling for a stairway, the moldings are joined at various angles, as in Fig. 7. This is known as varying miters, and a problem arises to find the miter angles. This is easily done by remembering that the miter angle is always half of the joint angle. To find the miter cut, that is the angle at which the miter cut is

47

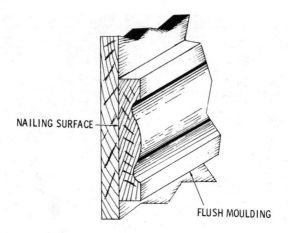

Fig. 4. Flush type molding.

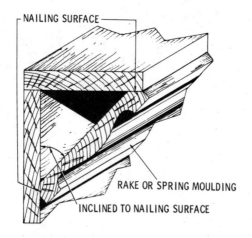

Fig. 5. Spring or rake type molding.

made, bisect the joint angle. This is done as shown in Fig. 8. The triangle *ABC* corresponds to the triangle *A* in Fig. 7. To find the miter cut at *A*, describe the arc *MS* of any radius with *A* as center. With *M* and *S* as centers, describe arcs *L* and *F*, intersecting at *R*. Draw line *AR*, which is the miter cut required.

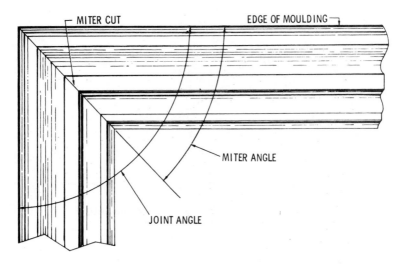

Fig. 6. Two pieces of flush molding joined at 90°.

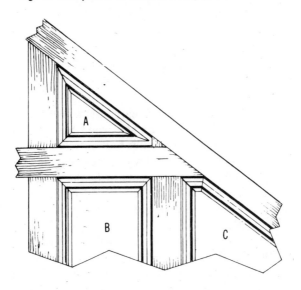

Fig. 7. Panel work of a wall illustrating varying miters. In panel (A) each angle is different, (B) both miters are equal, (C) has two different angles.

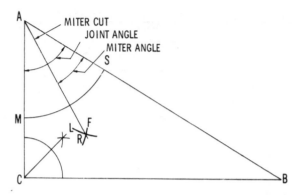

Fig. 8. A method of finding various miter cuts for different angles.

Mitering Spring Moldings

A spring molding is one that is made of thin material and is leaned or inclined away from the nailing surface, as shown in Fig. 5. These moldings are difficult to miter, especially when the joint is made with a gable, springs, or raking molding. The two most unusual forms of miters to cut on spring moldings are those on the inside and outside angles, as shown in Fig. 9. The pieces are represented as they would appear from the top sill looking down.

A difficult operation for most carpenters is the cutting of a spring molding when the horizontal portion has to miter with a gable or raking molding. The miter-box cuts for such joints are laid out as shown in Fig. 10. To lay out these cuts in constructing the miter box, make the "down cuts" *BB*, the same pitch as the plumb cut on the rake. The "over cuts," *OO* and *O'O'*, should be obtained as follows. Suppose a roof has a quarter pitch, find the rafter inclination, as in Fig. 11, by laying off *AB*=12 inch run and *BC*=6 inch rise, giving the roof angle *CAB* for ¼ pitch and rafter length *AC*=13.42 inch per foot run. With the setting 13.42 and 12, lay the steel square on top of the miter box, as shown in Fig. 12.

Mitering Panel and Raised Moldings

The following instructions illustrate how raised and rabbeted moldings may be cut and inserted in panels. Fig. 13 shows a

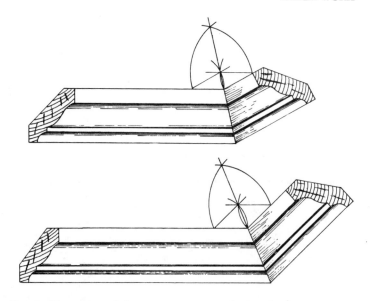

Fig. 9. Illustration of the two most unusual miter forms to cut.

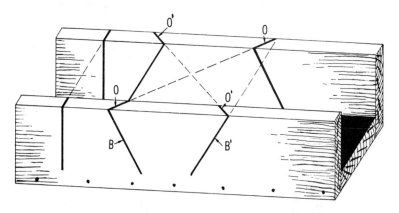

Fig. 10. Miter box layout for cutting a spring molding when the horizontal portion has to miter with a gable or raking molding.

panel and molding designed for a room or wardrobe door. *AB* denotes the outside frame, and *C,* the raised panel. *D* and *E* are the pine fillets inserted in the plowing, and *F* is the panel molding that has to be mitered around the inside edges of the frame.

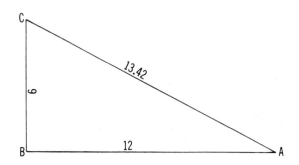

Fig. 11. Method of finding the angle for the cuts shown in Fig. 10.

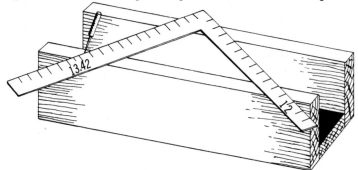

Fig. 12. Steel square applied to the miter box with 13.42 and 12
setting to mark for cuttings.

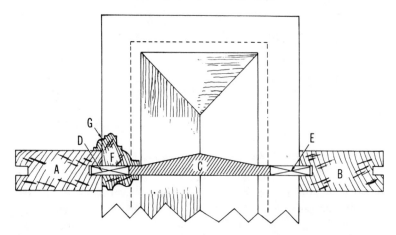

Fig. 13. Illustrating a panel and molding design.

Point *G* is the rabbet or lips on the molding *F*. If the framing *AB* is carefully constructed, and the surfaces are equal, the offset down to the panel will be equal all around, then all that is necessary is to make a hardwood strip or saddle equal in width to the depth of the offset.

The front door shown in Fig. 14 has both flush and raised panels. A raised 1-inch molding is on the outside or street side, and an ordinary ogee and chamfer is on the inside. The enlarged section is shown. This door is a good example of mitered moldings that form an attractive design. The difference between outside and inside miters must be explained—an *inside* miter is one in which the profile of the molding is contained, or rather the outside lines and highest parts are contained, within the angle of the framing. An *outside* miter is one that is directly opposite and not contained, but the whole of the molding is mitered on the

Fig. 14. End and side view of a door with raised molding.

panel outside the angle. Both miters are sawed similarly in the box with the exception of the reversing of the intersections.

Cutting Long Miters

In numerous instances, miter cuts must be made that cannot be cut in an ordinary or patent miter box. In such cases the work is facilitated by making a special box if there are several cuts of a kind to be made.

Fig. 15 shows a box 13 inches high and has a flare of 3¼ inches. Its construction requires miter cuts which cannot be made on an ordinary miter box. One corner is a rabbet joint, and the other corner is a miter joint. Each corner can be cut out by the use of an adjustable table power saw.

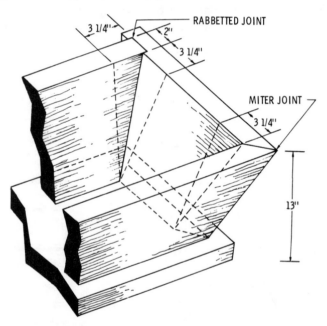

Fig. 15. A view of two joints, one showing a rabbet joint, and the other a miter joint.

Coping

By definition cope means to cover, or match against, a covering. Coping is generally used for moldings, the square and flat surfaces being fitted together, one piece abutting against the other. Against plaster, the inside miter is useless since one piece is almost certain to draw away and open the joint as it is being nailed into the studding. It can be mitered tightly enough by cutting the lengths a little full and springing them into place, but it is not advisable except possibly in solid corners. If against plastered walls, it may crack. The best way to make this joint is to cope it.

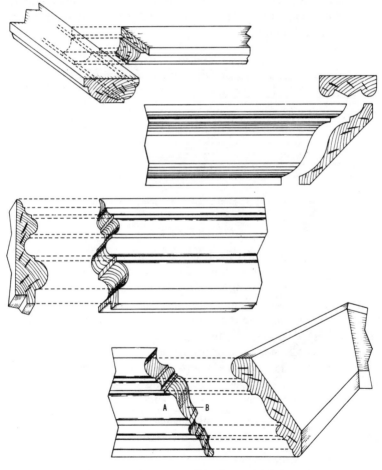

Fig. 16. Various styles of coped joints.

Fig. 16 shows various types of coped joints. In order to obtain this joint, the piece of molding is placed in a miter box and cut to a 45° angle. After this is done, the miter angle is cut by a coping saw along the design of the molding. If the corners are square, the miter and coped joints will fit perfectly.

Fig. 17 shows that when a molding is cut in a miter box for coping, it is always the reverse of the profile, and when cut out to the line thus formed, preferably with a coping saw, it fits to it at every inside corner so as to be invisible. In brief, each curved line and members join and intersect each to each without interruption at any point.

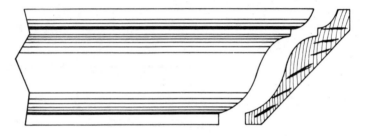

Fig. 17. Coped crown or spring molding.

SUMMARY

To make proper miter angles, a good miter box and back saw are needed. A carpenter can make a serviceable miter box from suitable hardwood for most of the common miter cuts.

In carpentry, various moldings are used. Some are designed to lay flat or flush against the surface, and others are shaped to lie inclined or at an angle to the surface.

Coping is another form of joining angles. After the molding is cut at a 45° angle, a coping saw is used to saw along the design of the adjoining molding. This is done to relieve any possible strain in molding corners on walls, such as plaster.

REVIEW QUESTIONS

1. What is a miter box?
2. What type of saw should be used in miter cuts?

3. What is coping?
4. What is spring or rake type molding?
5. Explain the difference between a rabbet joint and a miter joint.

CHAPTER 4

Doors

Doors, both exterior and interior, may also be considered flush, sash, or louver.

MANUFACTURED DOORS

For all practical purposes, doors can be obtained from the mill in stock sizes much cheaper than they can be made by hand. Stock sizes of doors cover a wide range, but those most commonly used are 2'4'' × 6'8'', 2'8'' × 6'8'', 3'0'' × 6'8'', and 3'0'' × 7'0''. These sizes are either 1⅜ (interior) or 1¾ (exterior) inches thick.

Sash (Paneled) Doors

Paneled, or sash, doors are made in a variety of ways, horizontal, vertical, and combinations of both. A sash door has for its component parts a top rail, bottom rail, and two stiles that form the sides of the door. Doors of the horizontal type have intermediate rails forming the panels; panels of the vertical type have horizontal rails and vertical stiles forming the panels (Figs. 1 and 2).

The rails and stiles of a door are generally mortised and tenoned, the mortise being cut in the side stiles as shown in Fig. 3. Top and bottom rails on paneled doors differ in width, the bottom rail being considerably wider. Intermediate rails are usually the same width as the top rail. Paneling material is usually plywood, which is set in grooves or dadoes in the stiles and rails, with the molding attached on most doors as a finish.

Fig. 1. Paneled or sash door.

Flush Doors

Flush doors are usually perfectly flat on both sides. Solid planks are rarely used for flush doors. Flush doors are made up with solid or hollow cores with two or more plies of veneer glued to the cores.

Solid-Core Doors

Solid-core doors are made of short pieces of wood glued together with the ends staggered very much like in brick laying. One or two plies of veneer are glued to the core. The first section, about ⅛ inch thick, is applied at right angles to the direction of the core, and the other section, ⅛ inch or less, is glued with the grain vertical. A ¾-inch strip, the thickness of the door, is glued to the edges of the door on all four sides. This type of door construction is shown in Fig. 4.

Colonial

Modern

Fig. 2. Several kinds of paneled doors.

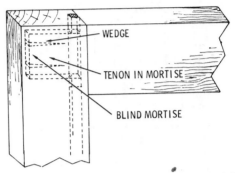

Fig. 3. Door construction showing mortise joints.

Hollow-Core Doors

Hollow-core doors, which are flush, have wooden grids or other honeycomb material for the base, with solid wood edging strips on all four sides. The face of this type door is usually 3-ply veneer instead of two single plies. The hollow-core door has a solid block on both sides for installing doorknobs and to permit the mortising of locks. The honeycomb-core door is for *interior* use only.

Louver Doors

This type of door has either stationary or adjustable louvers, and may be used as an interior door, room divider, or closet door. The louver door comes in many styles, such as those shown in Fig. 5. An exterior louver door may be used, which is called a *jalousie* door. This door has the adjustable louvers usually made of wood or glass. Although there is little protection against winter winds, a solid-type storm window is made to fit over the louvers to give added protection.

INSTALLING MILL-BUILT DOORS

There are numerous ways in which a door frame may be constructed. A door frame consists of the following essential parts.

1. Sill.
2. Threshold.
3. Side and top jamb.
4. Casing.

These parts are shown in Fig. 6.

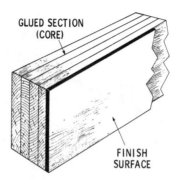

Fig. 4. Construction of a laminated or veneered door.

Fig. 5. Two styles of louver doors.

Door Frames

Before the exterior covering is placed on the outside walls, the door openings are prepared for the frames. To prepare the openings, square off any uneven pieces of sheathing and wrap heavy

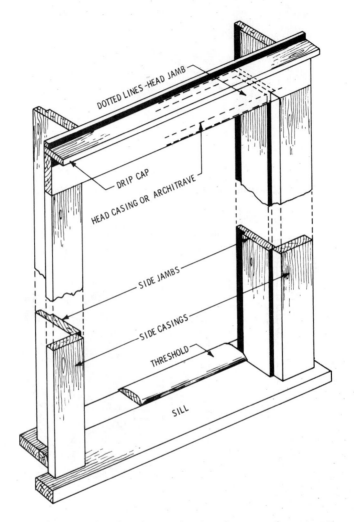

Fig. 6. View of a door frame showing the general construction.

building paper around the sides and top. Since the sill must be worked into a portion of the subflooring, no paper is put on the floor. Position the paper from a point even with the inside portion of the stud to a point about 6 inches on the sheathed walls, and tack it down with small nails.

Outside door frames are constructed in several ways. In more hasty constructions, there will be no door frame. The studs on each side of the opening act as the frame and the outside casing is applied to the walls before the door is hung. The inside door frame is constructed the same way as the outside frame.

Door Jambs

Door jambs are the lining to the framing of a door opening. Casings and stops are nailed to the jamb, and the door is securely fastened by hinges at one side. The width of the jamb will vary in accordance with the thickness of the walls. Door jambs are made and set in the following manner.

1. Regardless of how carefully the rough openings are made, be sure to plumb the jambs and level the heads when the jambs are set.
2. Rough openings are usually made $2^1/2$ inches larger each way than the size of the door to be hung. For example, a $2'8'' \times 6'8''$ door would need a rough opening of $2'10^1/2''$ $\times 6'10^1/2''$. This extra space allows for the jamb, the wedging, and the clearance space for the door to swing.
3. Level the floor across the opening to determine any variation in floor heights at the point where the jamb rests on the floor.
4. Cut the head jamb with both ends square, allowing for the width of the door plus the depth of both dadoes and a full $3/16$ inch for door clearance.
5. From the lower edge of the dado, measure a distance equal to the height of the door plus the clearance wanted at the bottom.
6. Do the same thing on the opposite jamb, only make additions or subtractions for the variation in the floor.
7. Nail the jambs and jamb heads together through the dado into the head jamb, as shown in Fig. 7.
8. Set the jambs into the opening and place small blocks under each jamb on the subfloor just as thick as the finish floor will be. This will allow the finish floor to go under the door.

9. Plumb the jambs and level the jamb head.
10. Wedge the sides to the plumb line with shingles between the jambs and the studs, and then nail securely in place.
11. Take care not to wedge the jambs unevenly.
12. Use a straightedge 5 to 6 feet long inside the jambs to help prevent uneven wedging.
13. Check each jamb and the head carefully. If a jamb is not plumb, it will have a tendency to swing the door open or shut, depending on the direction in which the jamb is out of plumb.

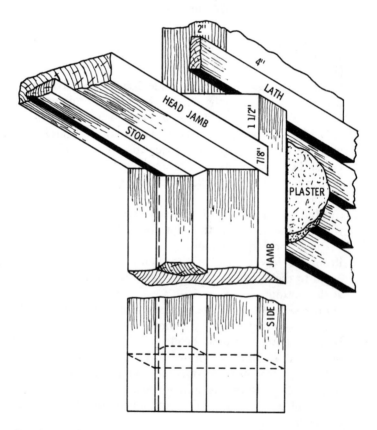

Fig. 7. Details showing the upper head jamb dadoed into the side jamb.

Door Trim

Door trim material is nailed onto the jambs to provide a finish between the jambs and the wall material. This is called *casing*. Sizes vary from $1/2$ to $3/4$ inch in thickness, and from $2 1/2$ to 6 inches in width. Most casing material has a concave back, to fit over uneven wall material. In miter work, care must be taken to make all joints clean, square, neat, and well fitted. If the trim is to be mitered at the top corners, a miter box, miter square, hammer, nail set, and block plane will be needed. Door openings are cased up in the following manner.

1. Leave a $1/4$-inch margin between the edge of the jamb and the casing on all sides.
2. Cut one of the side casings square and even with the bottom of the jamb.
3. Cut the top or mitered end next, allowing $1/4$ inch extra length for the margin at the top.
4. Nail the casing onto the jamb and set it even with the $1/4$-inch margin line, starting at the top and working toward the bottom.
5. The nails along the outer edge will need to be long enough to penetrate the casing and wall stud.
6. Set all nail heads about $1/8$ inch below the surface of the wood.
7. Apply the casing for the other side of the door opening in the same manner, followed by the head (or top) casing.

HANGING DOORS

If flush or sash doors are used, install them in the finished door opening as described below.

1. Cut off the stile extension, if any, and place the door in the frame. Plane the edges of the stiles until the door fits tightly against the hinge side and clears the lock side of the jamb about $1/16$ inch. Be sure that the top of the door fits squarely into the rabbeted recess and that the bottom swings free of the finished floor by about $1/2$ inch. The lock

stile of the door must be beveled slightly so that the edge of the door will not strike the edge of the door jamb.

2. After the proper clearance of the door has been made, set the door in position and place wedges as shown in Fig. 8. Mark the position of the hinges on the stile and on the jamb with a sharp pointed knife. The lower hinge must be placed slightly above the lower rail of the door. The upper hinge of the door must be placed slightly below the top rail in order to avoid cutting out a portion of the tenons of the door rails. There are three measurements to mark—the location of the hinge on the jamb, the location of the hinge on the door, and the thickness of the hinge on both the jamb and the door.

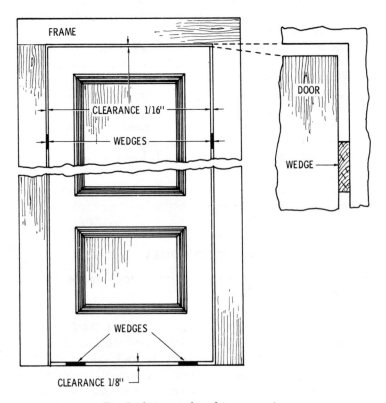

Fig. 8. Sizing a door for an opening.

3. Door butt hinges are designed to be mortised into the door and frame, as shown in Fig. 9. Fig. 10 shows a type of hinge that is installed directly to the door and jamb. Three hinges are usually used on full-length doors to prevent warping and sagging.
4. Using the butt as a pattern, mark the dimension of the butts on the door edge and the face of the jamb. The butts must fit snugly and exactly flush with the edge of the door and the face of the jamb. (A device called a butt marker can be helpful here.)

After placing the hinges and hanging the door, mark off the position for the lock and handle. The lock is generally placed about 36 inches from the floor level. Hold the lock in position on the stile and mark off with a sharp knife the area to be removed from the edge of the stile. Mark off the position of the doorknob hub. Bore out the wood to house the lock and chisel the mortises clean. After the lock assembly has been installed, close the door and mark the jamb for the striker plate.

SWINGING DOORS

Frequently, it is desirable to hang a door so that it opens as you pass through from either direction, yet remains closed at all other times. For this purpose, you can use swivel-style spring hinges. This type of hinge attaches to the rail of the door and to the jamb like an ordinary butt hinge. Another type is mortised into the bottom rail of the door and is fastened to the floor with a floor plate. In most cases, the floor-plate hinge, as shown in Fig. 11, is best because it will not weaken and let the door sag. It is also designed with a stop to hold the door open at right angles, if so desired.

SLIDING DOORS

Sliding doors are usually used for walk-in closets. They take up very little space, and they also allow a wide variation in floor plans. This type of door usually limits the access to a room or closet unless the doors are pushed back into a wall. Very few

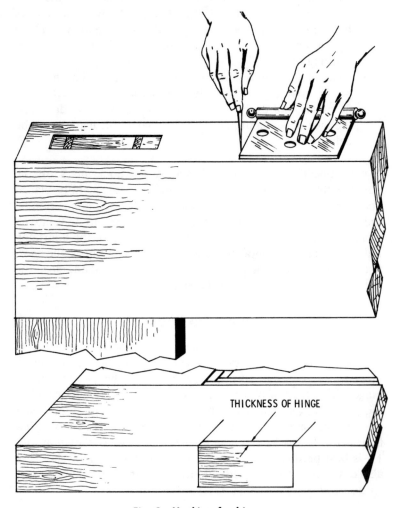

THICKNESS OF HINGE

Fig. 9. Marking for hinges.

sliding doors are pushed back into the wall because of the space and expense involved. Fig. 12 shows a double and a single sliding door track.

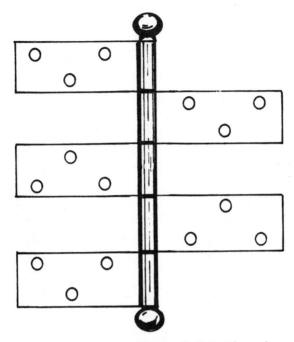

Fig. 10. New-type hinge is installed directly to the door and jamb.

GARAGE DOORS

Garage doors are made in a variety of sizes and designs. The principal advantage of any garage door is, of course, that it can be rolled up out of the way. In addition, the door cannot be blown shut due to wind, and it is not obstructed by snow and ice.

Standard residential garage doors are usually 9′ × 7′ for a single-car garage and 16′ × 7′ for a double. Residential-type garage doors are usually 1³/₄ inches thick.

When ordering doors for the garage, the following information should be forwarded to the manufacturer:

1. Width of opening between the finished jambs.
2. Height of the ceiling from the finished floor under the door to the underside of the finished header.
3. Thickness of the door.

71

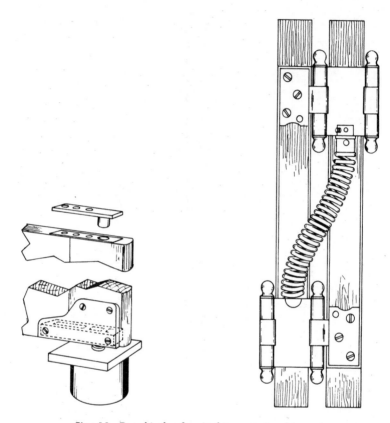

Fig. 11. Two kinds of swivel-type spring hinges.

4. Design of the door (number of glass windows and sections).
5. Material of jambs (they must be flush).
6. Headroom from the underside of the header to the ceiling, or to any pipes, lights, etc.
7. Distance between the sill and the floor level.
8. Proposed method of anchoring the horizontal track.
9. Depth to the rear from inside of the upper jamb.
10. Inside face width of the jamb buck, angle, or channel.

This information applies for overhead doors only; it does not apply to garage doors of the slide, folding, or hinged type. Doors

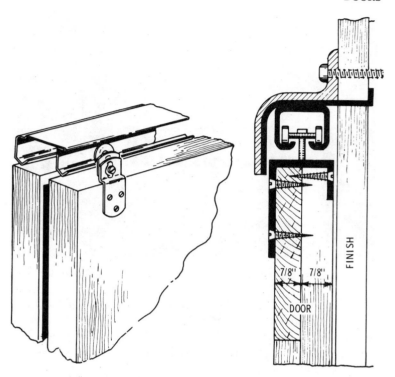

Fig. 12. Two types of sliding-door tracks.

can be furnished to match any style of architecture and may be provided with suitable size windows if desired (Fig. 13).

If your garage is attached to your house, the door often represents from one-third to one-fourth of the face of your house. Style and material should be considered to accomplish a pleasant effect with masonry or wood architecture. Fig. 14 shows three types of overhead garage doors that can be used with virtually any kind of architectural design. Many variations can be created from combinations of raised panels with routed or carved designs, as shown in Fig. 15. These panels may also be combined with plain raised panels to provide other dramatic patterns and color combinations.

Automatic garage-door openers were once a luxury item, but in the past few years the price has been reduced and failure

Fig. 13. Typical 18-foot overhead residential garage door.

minimized to the extent that many new installations include this feature. Automatic garage-door openers save time and eliminate the need to stop the car and get out in all kinds of weather. You also save the energy and effort required to open and close the door by hand.

The automatic door opener is a radio-activated motor-driven power unit that mounts on the ceiling of the garage and attaches to the inside top of the garage door. Electric impulses from a wall-mounted push button, or radio waves from a transmitter in your car, start the door mechanism. When the door reaches its limit of travel (up or down), the unit turns itself off and awaits the next command. Most openers on the market have a safety factor built in. If the door encounters an obstruction in its travel, it will instantly stop, or stop and reverse its travel. The door will not close until the obstruction has been removed. When the door is completely closed, it is automatically locked and cannot be opened from the outside, making it burglar resistant. Fig. 16 shows an automatic garage-door opener that can be quickly disconnected for manual-door operation in case of a power failure. The unit has a light, which turns on when the door opens to light up the inside of the garage.

(A) Fiberglass.

(B) Steel.

(C) Wood.

Fig. 14. Three types of garage doors.

SUMMARY

Most doors, both exterior and interior, are classified as sash, flush, or louver.

Sash doors are made in many styles. The rails and stiles are generally mortised and tenoned. Top and bottom rails on paneled doors differ in width, with the bottom rail considerably wider. The center rail is generally the same width as the top rail. The panel material is usually plywood, which is set in grooves or dadoes in the stiles and rails.

Fig. 15. Variations in carved or routed panel designs.

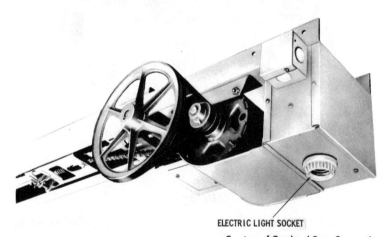

ELECTRIC LIGHT SOCKET

Courtesy of Overhead Door Corporation

Fig. 16. Typical automatic garage-door opener.

Flush doors, hollow and solid-core, generally all have the same appearance. The main difference in these is the method of construction. Solid-core doors are made of short pieces of wood glued together with the ends staggered very much like brick laying. Hollow-core doors have wooden grids or some type of honeycomb material for the base, with solid wood edging strips on all four sides. Glued to the cores of these doors are two or three layers of wood veneer, which make up the door panel. The honeycomb-core door is made for interior use only.

REVIEW QUESTIONS

1. Name the various type doors.
2. Why are honeycomb-core doors made for interior use only?
3. What is a door stop?
4. When hanging a door, how much clearance should there be at top, bottom, and sides?
5. How are solid-core doors constructed?

CHAPTER 5

Windows

The three main window types are gliding, double-hung, and casement, but there are also awning, bow, and bay windows (Fig. 1). Basic windows consist essentially of two parts, the frame and the sash. The frame is made up of four basic parts—the head, two jambs, and the sill. Good construction around the window frame is essential to good building. Where openings are to be provided, studding must be cut away and its equivalent strength replaced by doubling the studs on each side of the opening to form trimmers, and inserting a header at the top. If the opening is wide, the header should be doubled and trussed. At the bottom of the opening, a header or rough sill is inserted.

WINDOW FRAMING

This is the frame into which the window sash fits. It is set into a rough opening in the wall framing and is intended to hold the sash in place.

DOUBLE-HUNG WINDOWS

The double-hung window is made up of two parts—an upper and lower sash—which slide vertically past each other. A three-quarter view of a double-hung window is shown in Fig. 2. This type of window has some advantages and some disadvantages. Screens can be installed on the outside of the window without interfering with its operation. For full ventilation of a room, only one-half of the area of the window can be utilized,

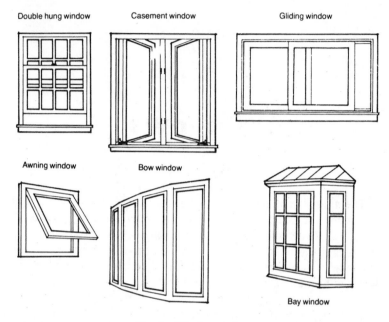

Double hung window   Casement window   Gliding window

Awning window   Bow window

Bay window

Fig. 1. Window styles.

and any current of air passing across its face is, to some extent, lost in the room. Double-hung windows are sometimes more involved in their frame construction and operation than is the casement window. Ventilation fans and air conditioners can be placed in the window with it partly closed.

HINGED OR CASEMENT WINDOWS

There are basically two types of casement windows—the outswinging and the inswinging. These windows may be hinged at the side, top, or bottom. The casement window that opens out requires the screen to be located on the inside. This type of window, when closed, is most efficient as far as waterproofing. The inswinging, like double-hung windows, are clear of screens, but they are extremely difficult to make watertight. Casement windows have the advantage of their entire area being opened to air currents, thus catching a parallel breeze and slanting it into a

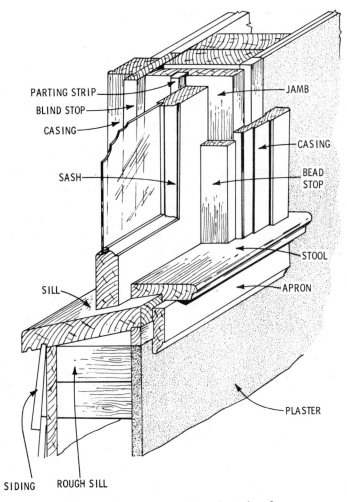

PARTING STRIP

BLIND STOP

CASING

SASH

JAMB

CASING

BEAD STOP

STOOL

APRON

SILL

PLASTER

SIDING   ROUGH SILL

Fig. 2. Three-quarter view of window frame.

room. Casement windows are considerably less complicated in their construction than double-hung units. Sill construction is very much like that for a double-hung window, however, but with the stool much wider and forming a stop for the bottom rail. When there are two casement windows in a row in one frame, they are separated by a vertical double jamb called a mullion, or the stiles may come together in pairs like a french door. The edges of the stiles may be a reverse rabbet, a beveled reverse rabbet with battens, or beveled astrogals. The battens and astrogals ensure better weathertightness.

GLIDING, BOW, BAY, AND AWNING WINDOWS

Gliding windows consist of two sash that slide horizontally right or left. They are often installed high up in a home to provide light and ventilation without sacrificing privacy.

Awning windows have a single sash hinged at the top and open outward from the bottom. They are often used at the bottom of a fixed picture window to provide ventilation without obstructing the view. They are popular in ranch homes.

Bow and bay windows add architectural interest to a home. Bow windows curve gracefully, while bay windows are straight across the middle and angled at the ends. They are particularly popular in Georgian and Colonial homes.

As noted in Volume 3 of *Carpenters and Builders Library,* windows play an important role in how energy-tight your house is.

First, experts agree that wood windows are better than metal ones for insulation purposes, simply because metal conducts heat better than wood. But even more important is double glazing, which contains a dead air space that inhibits heat escaping—or getting in, should you have air conditioning. The second pane can be incorporated in the window, as shown in Fig. 3, or it can be removable. If you live in an area where heating costs are very high, consider triple glazing—three panes of glass with air spaces between. Tinted or reflective glass is good for warding off the sun's rays in warmer climates.

WINDOW SASH

Most windows are normally composed of an upper and a lower sash. These sash slide up and down, swing in or out, or may be stationary. There are two general types of wood sash— fixed or permanent, and movable. Fixed window sash are removable only with the aid of a carpenter. Movable sash may be

Fig. 3. Insulated glass.

of the variety that slides up and down in channels in the frame, called *double-hung*. Casement-type windows swing in or out and are hinged on the sides. Some sliding sash are counterbalanced by weights, called *sash weights,* their actual weight equal to one-half that of each sash, or there may be some friction hardware. Sash are classified according to the number of lights—single or double.

Sash Installation

Place the upper double-hung sash in position and trim off a slight portion of the top rail to ensure a good fit, and tack the upper sash in position. Fit the lower sash in position by trimming off the sides. Place the lower sash in position, and trim off a sufficient amount from the bottom rail to permit the meeting rails to meet on a level. In most cases, the bottom rail will be trimmed on an angle to permit the rail and sill to match both inside and outside, as shown in Fig. 4.

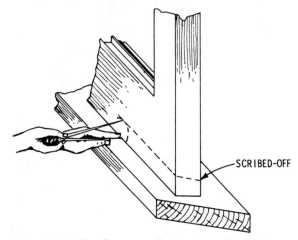

—SCRIBED-OFF

Fig. 4. Marking bottom rail trim to match sill plate.

Sash Weights

If sash weights are used, remove each sash after it has been properly cut and sized. Select sash weights equal to one-half the weight of each sash and place in position in the weight pockets. Measure the proper length of sash cord for the lower sash and attach it to the stiles and weights on both sides. Adjust the length of the cord so that the weight will not strike the pulley or bottom of the frame when the window is moved up and down. Install the cords and weights for the upper sash and adjust the cord so that the weights run smoothly. Close the pockets in the frame and install the blind stop, parting strip, and bead stop.

There are many other types of window lifts, such as spring-loaded steel tapes, spring-tension metal guides, and full-length coil springs.

GLAZING SASH

The panes of glass, or *lights,* as they are called, are generally cut ⅛ inch smaller on all four sides to allow for irregularities in cutting and in the sash. This leaves an approximate margin of $1/16$ inch between the edge of the glass and the sides of the rabbet. Fig. 5 shows two lights or panes of glass in position for glazing. To install the window glass properly, first spread a film of glazing compound close to the edge on the inside portion of the glass. After the glass has been inserted, drive or press in at least two glazier points on each side. This is illustrated in Fig. 6.

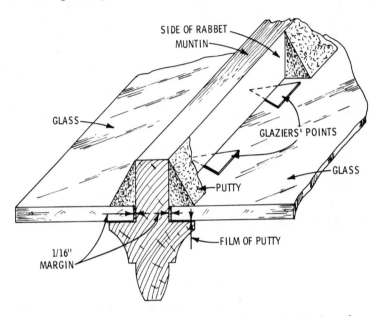

Fig. 5. The glazier points that are removed to replace broken glass.

When the glass is firmly secured with the glazier points, the compound (which is soft) is put on around the glass with a putty knife beveled as shown in Fig. 6. Do not project the compound beyond the edge of the rabbet so that it will be visible from the other side.

SHUTTERS

In coastal areas where damaging high winds occur frequently, shutters are necessary to protect large plate-glass windows from being broken. The shutters are mounted on hinges and can be closed at a moment's notice. Throughout the Midwest, shutters are generally installed for decoration only and are mounted

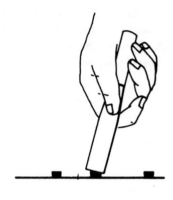

Fig. 6. Push glazier's points in with putty knife.

stationary to the outside wall. There are generally two types of shutters—the solid panel, and the slat or louver type. Louver shutters can have stationary or movable slats.

SUMMARY

Many styles and sizes of windows are used in various house designs, but the main ones are gliding, double-hung, and casement. A window consists generally of two parts, the frame and the sash.

Good construction around window frames is essential to good building. Where window openings are to be provided, studding must be cut and its equivalent strength replaced by doubling the studs on each side of the opening. The top and bottom of each opening must have a double header to add strength. The rough window opening is generally made at least 10 inches larger each way than the window glass size. This extra 10-inch allowance provides room for weights, springs, or balances.

Double-hung windows are made up of two parts—the upper and lower sash, which slide vertically past each other. Only one-half of the area of the window can be used for ventilation, which is a disadvantage.

REVIEW QUESTIONS

1. Name the various window classifications.
2. What size should the rough opening be for a double-hung window?
3. What are some advantages of casement windows?
4. Name a few advantages in using window shutters.
5. What are glazier points, and why should they be used when installing window glass?

CHAPTER 6

Sheathing and Siding

Sheathing is nailed directly to the framework of the building. Its purpose is to strengthen the building, to provide a base material to which finish siding can be attached, to act as insulation, and in some cases to be a base for further insulation. Some of the common types of sheathing include fiberboard, wood, and plywood.

FIBERBOARD SHEATHING

Fiberboard usually comes in 2×8 or 4×8 sheets that are tongue-and-grooved and generally coated or impregnated with an asphalt material that increases water resistance. Thickness is normally $1/2$ and $25/32$ inch, and may be used where the stud spacing does not exceed 16 inches. Fiberboard sheathing should be nailed with 2-inch galvanized roofing nails or other type of noncorrosive nails. If the fiberboard is used as sheathing, most builders will use plywood at all corners (the thickness of the sheathing) to strengthen the walls, as shown in Fig. 1.

WOOD SHEATHING

Wood wall sheathing can be obtained in almost all widths, lengths, and grades. Generally, widths are from 6 to 12 inches, with lengths selected for economical use. Almost all solid wood wall sheathing used is $25/32$ to 1 inch in thickness. This material may be nailed on horizontally or diagonally, as shown in Fig. 2. Wood sheathing is laid on tight, with all joints made over the studs. If the sheathing is to be put on horizontally, it should be

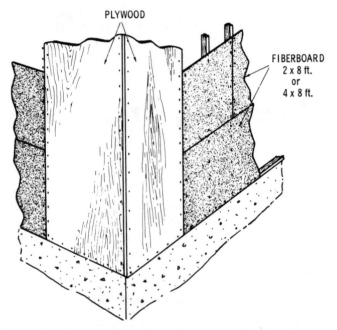

PLYWOOD

FIBERBOARD
2 x 8 ft.
or
4 x 8 ft.

Fig. 1. Method of using plywood on all corners as bracing when using fiberboard as exterior sheathing.

started at the foundation and worked toward the top. If the sheathing is installed diagonally, it should be started at the corners of the building and worked toward the center or middle.

Diagonal sheathing should be applied at a 45° angle. This method of sheathing adds greatly to the rigidity of the wall and eliminates the need for the corner bracing. It also provides an excellent tie to the sill plate when it is installed diagonally. There is more lumber waste than with horizontal sheathing because of the angle cut, and the application is somewhat more difficult. Fig. 3 shows the wrong way and the correct way of laying diagonal sheathing.

PLYWOOD SHEATHING

Plywood as a wall sheathing is good sheathing because of its size, weight, and stability, plus the ease and rapidity of installa-

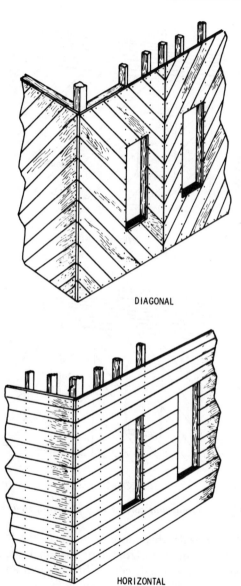

DIAGONAL

HORIZONTAL

Fig. 2. Two methods of nailing on wood sheathing.

91

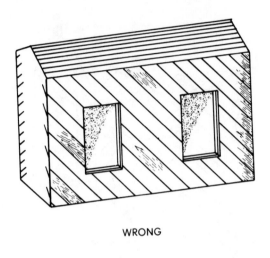

WRONG

CORRECT

Fig. 3. Wrong and correct way of laying sheathing.

tion. It adds considerably more strength to the frame structure than the conventional horizontal or diagonal sheathing. When plywood sheathing is used, corner bracing can also be omitted. Large-size panels effect a major saving in the time required for application and still provide a tight, draft-free installation that contributes a high insulation value to the walls. Minimum thickness of plywood wall sheathing is $5/16$ inch for 16-inch stud spacing, and $3/8$ inch for 24-inch stud spacing. The panels should be installed with the face grain parallel to the studs. However, a little more stiffness can be obtained by installing them across the studs, but this requires more cutting and fitting. Nail spacing should not be more than 6 inches on center at the edges of the panels and not more than 12 inches on center elsewhere. Joints should meet on the centerline of framing members.

Urethane and Fiberglass

With the accent in recent years on energy saving, a number of other insulations have been developed that have fairly high insulating value. For example, there is urethane, $1^{1}/4$-inch-thick material that, when combined with regular insulation, yields an R factor of 22 (Fig. 4). There is also fiberglass insulation with an R-4.8 (Fig. 5). Such insulations are particuarly good on masonry construction because brick itself has very little insulating value and requires whatever insulation can be built in.

SHEATHING PAPER

Sheathing paper should be used on a frame structure when wood or plywood sheathing is used. It should be water resistant but not vapor resistant. It should be applied horizontally, starting at the bottom of the wall. Succeeding layers should lap about 4 inches, and lap over strips around openings. Strips about 6 inches wide should be installed behind all exterior trim or exterior openings.

WOOD SIDING

One of the materials most characteristic of the exteriors of American houses is wood siding. The essential properties required for wood siding are good painting characteristics, easy working qualities, and freedom from warp. These properties are present to a high degree in the cedars, eastern white pine, sugar pine, western white pine, cypress, and redwood.

Material used for exterior siding should preferably be of a select grade, and should be free from knots, pitch pockets, and

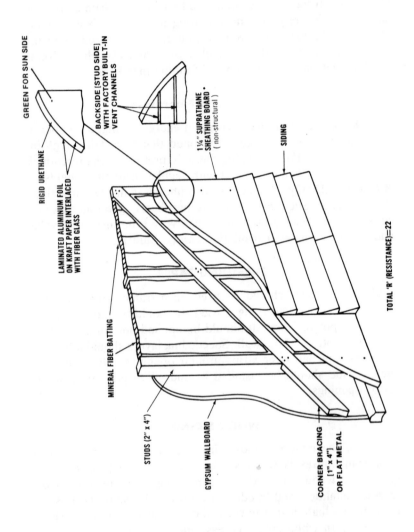

GREEN FOR SUN SIDE

BACKSIDE (STUD SIDE) WITH FACTORY BUILT-IN VENT CHANNELS

RIGID URETHANE

LAMINATED ALUMINUM FOIL ON KRAFT PAPER INTERLACED WITH FIBER GLASS

1¼" SUPRATHANE SHEATHING BOARD * (non-structural)

SIDING

TOTAL 'R' (RESISTANCE)=22

MINERAL FIBER BATTING

STUDS (2" x 4")

GYPSUM WALLBOARD

CORNER BRACING (1" x 4") OR FLAT METAL

Fig. 4. Rigid urethane, when combined with other wall elements, yields an R-22 insulation factor.

wavy edges. The moisture content at the time of application should be that which it would attain in service. This would be approximately 12 percent, except in the dry southwestern states, where the moisture content should average about 9 percent.

Fig. 5. Fiberglass sheathing alone has an R-4.8 insulation factor. Courtesy of Owens-Corning.

Bevel Siding

Plain bevel siding, as shown in Fig. 6, is made in nominal 4-, 5-, and 6-inch widths with $7/16$-inch butts, 6-, 8-, and 10-inch widths with $9/16$- and $11/16$-inch butts. Bevel siding is generally furnished in random lengths varying from 4 to 20 feet in length.

Drop siding is generally $3/4$ inch thick and is made in a variety of patterns with either matched or shiplap edges. Fig. 7 shows three common patterns of drop siding that are applied horizontally. Fig. 7A may be applied vertically, for example at the gable ends of a house. Drop siding was designed to be applied directly to the studs, and it thereby serves as sheathing and exterior wall covering. It is widely used in this manner in farm structures,

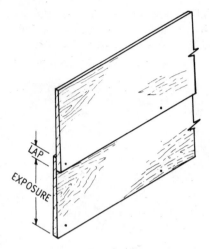

Fig. 6. Bevel siding.

such as sheds and garages, in all parts of the country. When used over or when in contact with other material, such as sheathing or sheathing paper, water may work through the joints and be held between the sheathing and the siding. This sets up a condition conducive to paint failure and decay. Such problems can be avoided when the side walls are protected by a good roof overhang.

Square-Edge Siding

Square-edge or clapboard siding made of $^{25}/_{32}$-inch board is occasionally selected for architectural effects. In this case, wide boards are generally used. Some of this siding is also beveled on the back at the top to allow the boards to lie rather close to the sheathing, thus providing a solid nailing surface.

Vertical Siding

Vertical siding is commonly used on the gable ends of a house, over entrances, and sometimes for large wall areas. The type used may be plain-surfaced matched boards, patterned matched boards, or square-edge boards covered at the joint with a batten strip. Matched vertical siding should preferably not be more than 8 inches wide and should have 2 eight-penny nails not more

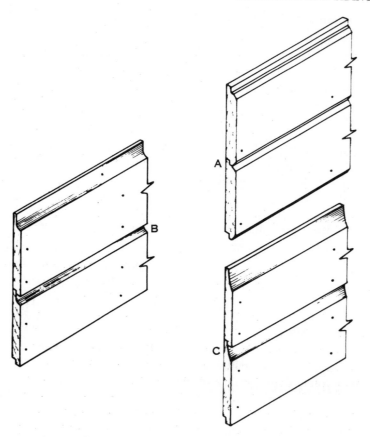

Fig. 7. Types of drop siding (A) V-rustic, (B) drop, (C) rustic drop.

than 4 feet apart. Backer blocks should be placed between studs to provide a good nailing base. The bottom of the boards should be undercut to form a water drip.

Batten-type siding is often used with wide square-edged boards, which, because of their width, are subjected to considerable expansion and contraction. The batten strips used to cover the joints should be nailed to only one siding board so the adjacent board can swell and shrink without splitting the boards or the batten strip.

97

Plywood Siding

Plywood is often used in gable ends, sometimes around windows and porches, and occasionally as an overall exterior wall covering. The sheets are made either plain or with irregularly cut striations. It can be applied horizontally or vertically. The joints can be molded batten, V-grooves, or flush. Sometimes it is installed as lap siding. Plywood siding should be of exterior grade, since houses are often built with little overhang of the roof, particularly on the gable end. This permits rain water to run down freely over the face of the siding. For unsheathed walls, the following thicknesses are suggested:

Minimum thickness	Maximum stud space
$^3/_8$ inch	16 inches on center
$^1/_2$ inch	20 inches on center
$^5/_8$ inch	24 inches on center

Treated Siding

Houses are often built with little or no overhang of the roof, particularly on the gable ends. This permits rain water to run down freely over the face of the siding. Under such conditions water may work up under the laps in bevel siding or through joints in drop siding by capillary action, and provide a source of moisture that may cause paint blisters or peeling.

A generous application of a water repellent preservative to the back of the siding will be quite effective in reducing capillary action with bevel siding. In drop siding, the treatment would be applied to the matching edges. Dipping the siding in the water repellent would be still more effective. The water repellent should be applied to all end cuts, at butt points, and where the siding meets door and window trim.

Wood Shingles and Shakes

Cedar shingles and shakes are also available. They come in a variety of grades and may be applied in several ways. You may get them in random widths 18 to 24 inches long or in a uniform

18 inches. The shingles may be installed on regular sheathing or on an undercourse of shingles, which produces a shadowed effect. Cedar, of course, stands up to the weather well and does not have to be painted.

Asbestos Shingles

These shingles offer good economy, though they are brittle and tend to break easily if hit. They come in various colors and are installed by driving nails through predrilled holes on a 15-lb. felt base. It is best to use a shingle cutter when installing asbestos shingles.

INSTALLATION OF SIDING

The spacing for siding should be carefully laid out before the first board is applied. The bottom of the board that passes over the top of the first-floor windows should coincide with the top of the window cap, as shown in Fig. 8. To determine the maximum board spacing or exposure, deduct the minimum lap from the overall width of the siding. The number of board spaces between the top of the window and the bottom of the first course at the foundation wall should be such that the maximum exposure will not be exceeded. This may mean that the boards will have less than the maximum exposure.

Siding starts with the bottom course of boards at the foundation, as shown in Fig. 9. Sometimes the siding is started on a water table, which is a projecting member at the top of the foundation to throw off water, as shown in Fig. 10. Each succeeding course overlaps the upper edge of the lower course. The minimum head lap is 1 inch for 4- and 6-inch widths, and $1^1/_4$-inch lap for widths over 6 inches. The joints between boards in adjacent courses should be staggered as much as possible. Butt joints should always be made on a stud, or where boards butt against window and door casings and corner boards. The siding should be carefully fitted and be in close contact with the member or adjacent pieces. Some carpenters fit the boards so tight that they have to spring the boards in place, which assures a tight joint. Loose-fitting joints allow water to get behind the siding thereby causing paint deterioration around the joints and seting up conditions conducive to decay at the ends of the siding.

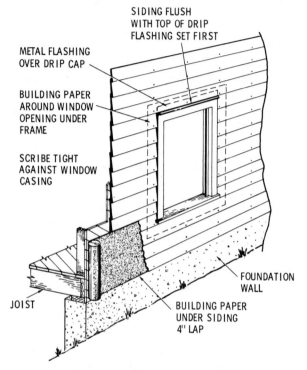

Fig. 8. Installation of bevel siding.

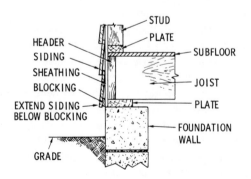

Fig. 9. Installation of the first or bottom course.

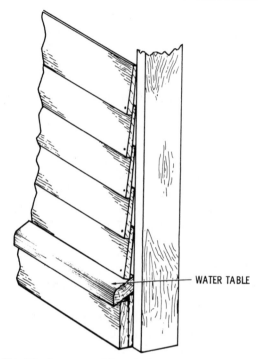

Fig. 10. A water table, which is sometimes used.

WATER TABLE

Types of Nails

Nails cost very little compared to the cost of siding and labor, but the use of good nails is important. It is poor economy to buy siding that will last for years and then use nails that will rust badly within a few years. Rust-resistant nails will hold the siding permanently and will not disfigure light-colored paint surfaces.

There are two types of nails commonly used with siding, one having a small head and the other a slightly larger head. The small-head casing nail is set (driven with a nailset) about $1/16$ inch below the surface of the siding. The hole is filled with putty after the prime coat of paint is applied. The large-head nail is driven flush with the face of the siding, with the head being later covered with paint. Ordinary steel wire nails tend to rust in a short time and cause a disfiguring stain on the face of the siding.

In some cases, the small-head nail will show rust spots through the putty and paint. Noncorrosive-type nails (galvanized, aluminum, and stainless steel) that will not cause rust stains are readily available.

Bevel siding should be face nailed to each stud with noncorrosive nails, the size depending upon the thickness of the siding and the type of sheathing used. The nails are generally placed about ½ inch above the butt edge, in which case they pass through the upper edge of the lower course of siding. Another method recommended for bevel siding by most associations representing siding manufacturers is to drive the nails through the siding just above the lap so that the nail misses the thin edge of the piece of siding underneath. The latter method permits expansion and contraction of the siding board with seasonal changes in moisture content.

Corner Treatment

The method of finishing the wood siding at the exterior corners is influenced somewhat by the overall house design. Corner boards are appropriate to some designs, and mitered joints to others. Wood siding is commonly joined at the exterior corners by corner boards, mitered corners, or metal corners.

Corner Boards—Corner boards, as shown in Fig. 11, are used with bevel or drop siding and are generally made of nominal 1- or 1¼-inch material, depending upon the thickness of the siding. It may be either plain or molded, depending on the architectural treatment of the house. The corner boards may be applied vertically against the sheathing, with the siding fitting tightly against the narrow edge of the corner board. The joints between the siding and the corner boards and trim should be calked or treated with a water repellent. Corner boards and trim around windows and doors are sometimes applied over the siding, a method that minimizes the entrance of water into the ends of the siding.

Mitered Corners—Mitered corners, such as shown in Fig. 12, must fit tightly and smoothly for the full depth of the miter. To maintain a tight fit at the miter, it is important that the siding is properly seasoned before delivery, and is stored at the site so as to be protected from rain. The ends should be set in white lead

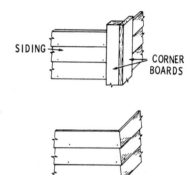

Fig. 11. Corner treatment for bevel siding using the corner board.

Fig. 12. Illustrating the mitered corner treatment.

when the siding is applied, and the exposed faces should be primed immediately after it is applied. At interior corners, shown in Fig. 13, the siding is butted against a corner strip of nominal 1- or 1¼-inch material, depending upon the thickness of the siding.

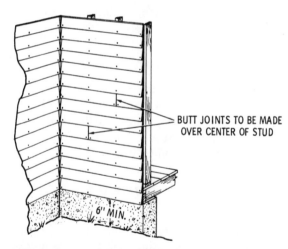

Fig. 13. Illustrating the construction of an interior corner using bevel siding.

Metal Corners—Metal corners, as shown in Fig. 14, are made of 8-gauge metals, such as aluminum and galvanized iron. They are used with bevel siding as a substitute for mitered corners, and can be purchased at most lumberyards. The application of metal corners takes less skill than is required to make good mitered corners, or to fit the siding to a corner board. Metal corners should always be set in white lead paint.

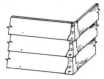

Fig. 14. Corner treatment for bevel siding using the corner metal caps.

METAL SIDING

The metal most popular of those used in siding is aluminum. It is installed over most types of sheathing with an aluminum building paper (for insulation) nailed on between the sheathing and siding or insulation built onto the siding. Its most attractive characteristic is the long-lasting finish. The cost of painting and maintenance has made this type of siding doubly attractive. Aluminum siding can be installed over old siding that has cracked and weathered, or where paint will not hold up.

VINYL SIDING

Also popular is vinyl siding (Fig. 15). This comes in a wide variety of colors, textures, and styles. As with aluminum siding, the big advantage of vinyl siding is that it does not need to be painted and will not corrode, dent, or pit. It is relatively susceptible to cracking if hit when it is very cold.

SUMMARY

Sheathing is nailed directly to the framework of the building. The purpose of sheathing is to strengthen the structure, to provide a nailing base for siding, and to act as insulation. Types of sheathing include fiberboard, wood, plywood, urethane, and fiberglass.

Fiberboard is generally furnished in 2′ × 8′ or 4′ × 8′ sheets and is usually coated with an asphalt material to make it waterproof. When fiberboard sheathing is used, most builders will use plywood at all corners to strengthen the walls. Fiber-

Fig. 15. Solid vinyl siding comes in various colors and textures. It never needs to be painted.

board is normally ½ or $^{25}/_{32}$ inch thick and generally tongue-and-grooved.

Wood sheathing is generally any size from 1″ × 6″ to 1″ × 12″ in width. The material may be installed horizontally or diagonally with all joints made over a stud. Diagonal sheathing should be applied at a 45° angle. This adds greatly to the rigidity of the walls and eliminates the need for corner bracing. More lumber waste is realized than when applying horizontal sheathing, but an excellent tie to the sill plate is accomplished when installed diagonally.

One of the most popular exterior wall finishes of American houses is wood siding. Various types or styles include bevel, drop, square-edge, and vertical siding. A number of methods are used as a corner treatment when using wood bevel siding. Some corners are designed to use a vertical corner board, which is generally 1- or 1¼-inch material. Mitered corners are sometimes used, or the same effect can be obtained by using metal corners.

Of the metal sidings, aluminum is the most popular.

REVIEW QUESTIONS

1. What is fiberboard and how is it used as sheathing?
2. What are some advantages in using wood sheathing placed diagonally?
3. Name the various styles of wood siding.
4. How are corners on wood siding treated?
5. What is a water table?

CHAPTER 7

Stairs

All craftsmen who have tried to build stairs have found it (like boat building) to be an art in itself. This chapter is not intended to discourage the builder but to impress on him the fact that unless he first masters the principle of stair layout, he will have many difficulties in the construction. Although stair building is a branch of mill work, the carpenter should know the principles of simple stair layout and construction because he is often called upon to construct porch steps, basement and attic stairs, and other stairs. In order to follow the instructions intelligently, the carpenter should be familiar with the terms and names of parts used in stair building.

STAIR CONSTRUCTION

Stairways should be designed, arranged, and installed so as to afford safety, adequate headroom, and space for the passage of furniture. In general, there are two types of stairs in a house—those serving as principal stairs and those used as service stairs. The principal stairs are designed to provide ease and comfort and are often made a feature of design, while the service stairs leading to the basement or attic are usually somewhat steeper and constructed of less expensive materials.

Stairs may be built in place, or they may be built as units in the shop and set in place. Both methods have their advantages and disadvantages, and custom varies with locality. Stairways may have a straight continuous run, with or without an intermediate platform, or they may consist of two or more runs at angles to each other. In the best and safest practice, a platform is introduced at the angle, but the turn may be made by radiating risers called *winders*. Nonwinder stairways are most frequently encountered in residential planning because winder stairways represent a condition generally regarded as undesirable. However, use of winders is sometimes necessary because of cramped space. In such instances, winders should be adjusted to replace landings so that the width of the tread 18 inches from the narrow converging end will not be less than the tread width on the straight run.

RATIO OF RISER TO TREAD

There is a definite relationship between the height of a riser and the width of a tread, and all stairs should be laid out to conform to the well-established rules governing this relationship. If the combination of run and rise is too great, the steps are tiring, placing a strain on the leg muscles and on the heart. If the steps are too short, the foot may kick the leg riser at each step, and an attempt to shorten the stride may be tiring. Experience has proved that a riser 7 to 7½ inches high, with appropriate tread, combines both comfort and safety, and these limits therefore determine the standard height of risers commonly used for principal stairs. Service stairs may be narrow and steeper than the principal stairs, and are often unduly so, but it is well not to exceed 8 inches for the risers.

As the height of the riser is increased, the width of the tread must be decreased for comfortable results. A very good ratio is provided by either of the following rules, which are exclusive of the nosing:

1. Tread plus twice the riser equals 25.
2. Tread multiplied by the riser equals 75.

A riser of 7½ inches would, therefore, require a tread of 10 inches, and a riser of 6½ inches would require a tread 12 inches wide. Treads are rarely made less than 9 inches or more than 12 inches wide. The treads of main stairs should be made of prefinished hardwood.

DESIGN OF STAIRS

The location and the width of a stairway (together with the platforms) having been determined, the next step is to fix the height of the riser and width of the tread. After a suitable height of riser is chosen, the exact distance between the finish floors of the two stories under consideration is divided by the riser height. If the answer is an *even* number, the number of risers is thereby determined. It very often happens that the result is *uneven,* in which case the story height is divided by the whole number next above or below the quotient. The result of this division gives the height of the riser. The tread is then proportioned by one of the rules for ratio of riser to tread.

Assume that the total height from one floor to the top of the next floor is 9'6'', or 114 inches, and that the riser is to be approximately 7½ inches. The 114 inches would be divided by 7½ inches, which would give $15^1/_5$ risers. However, the number of risers must be an *equal or whole* number. Since the nearest whole number is 15, it may be assumed that there are to be 15 risers, in which case 114 divided by 15 equals 7.6 inches, or approximately $7^9/_{16}$ inches for the height of each riser. To determine the width of the tread, multiply the height of the riser by 2 ($2 \times 7^9/_{16} = 15\frac{1}{8}$), and deduct 25 ($25 - {}^{15}/_{18} = 9\frac{7}{8}$ inches).

The headroom is the vertical distance from the top of the tread to the underside of the flight or ceiling above, as shown in Fig. 1. Although it varies with the steepness of the stairs, the minimum allowed would be 6'8''.

FRAMING OF STAIRWELL

When large openings are made in the floor, such as for a stairwell, one or more joists must be cut. The location in the floor has a direct bearing on the method of framing the joists.

The principles explained in Chapter 8 of *Carpenters and Builders Library,* Vol. 3, may be referred to in considering the framing around openings in floors for stairways. The framing members around these openings are generally of the same depth as the joists. Fig. 2 shows the typical framing around a stairwell and landing.

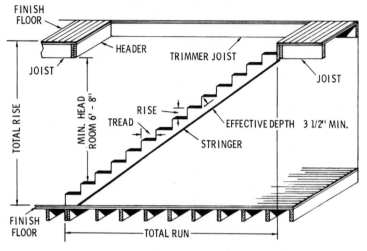

Fig. 1. Stairway design.

The headers are the short beams at right angles to the regular joists at the end of the floor opening. They are doubled and support the ends of the joists that have been cut off. Trimmer joists are at the sides of the floor opening and run parallel to the regular joists. They are also doubled and support the ends of the headers. Tail joists are joists that run from the headers to the bearing position.

STRINGERS OR CARRIAGES

The treads and risers are supported upon stringers or carriages that are solidly fixed in place and are level and true on the framework of the building. The stringers may be cut or ploughed to fit the outline of the tread and risers. The third stringer should be installed in the middle of the stairs when the treads are less than $1^1/_8$ inches thick and the stairs are more than 2' 2'' wide. In some cases, rough stringers are used during the construction period. These have rough treads nailed across the stringers for the convenience of workmen until the wall finish is applied. There are several forms of stringers classed according to the method of attaching the risers and treads. These different types are *cleated, cut, built-up,* and *rabbeted.*

110

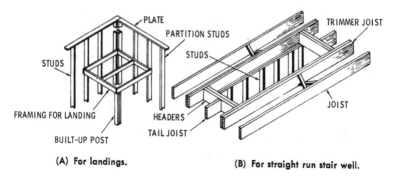

(A) For landings. (B) For straight run stair well.

Fig. 2. Framing of stairways.

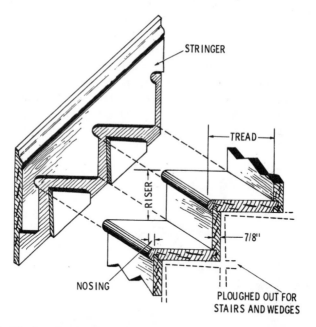

Fig. 3. The housing in the stringer board for the tread and riser.

When the wall finish is complete, the finish stairs are erected or built in place. This work is generally done by a stair builder, who is a specialist, but the carpenter also does the job. The wall stringer may be ploughed out, or rabbeted, as shown in Fig. 3, to

111

the exact profile of the tread, riser, and nosing, with sufficient space at the back to take the wedges. The top of the riser is tongued into the front of the tread and into the bottom of the next riser. The wall stringer is spiked to the inside of the wall, and the treads and risers are fitted together and forced into the wall stringer nosing, where they are set tight by driving and gluing the wood wedges behind them. The wall stringer shows above the profiles of the tread and riser as a finish against the wall and is often made continuous with the baseboard of the upper and lower landing. If the outside stringer is an open stringer, it is cut out to fit the risers and treads and nailed against the outside carriage. The edges of the riser are mitered with the corresponding edges of the stringer, and the nosing of the tread is returned upon its outside edge along the face of the stringer. Another method would be to butt the stringer to the riser and cover the joint with an inexpensive stair bracket.

Fig. 4 shows a finish stringer nailed in position on the wall, and the rough carriage nailed in place against the stringer. If there are walls on both sides of the staircase, the other stringer and carriage would be located in the same way. The risers are nailed to the riser cuts of the carriage on each side and butt

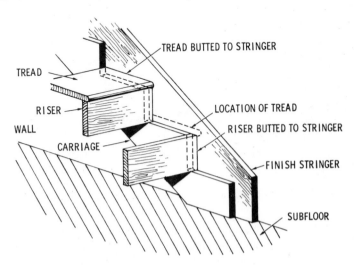

Fig. 4. Finished wall stringer and carriage.

against each side of the stringer. The treads are nailed to the tread cuts of the carriage and butt against the stringer. This is the least expensive of the types described and perhaps the best construction to use when the treads and risers are to be nailed to the carriages.

Another method of fitting the treads and risers to the wall stringers is shown in Fig. 5A. The stringers are laid out with the

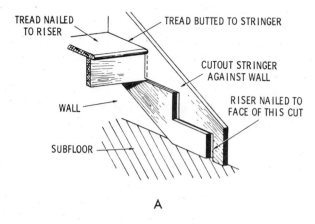

TREAD NAILED TO RISER

TREAD BUTTED TO STRINGER

CUTOUT STRINGER AGAINST WALL

RISER NAILED TO FACE OF THIS CUT

WALL

SUBFLOOR

A

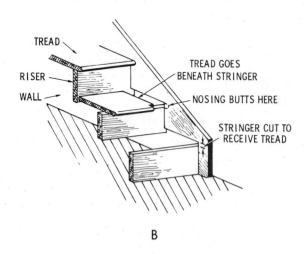

TREAD

RISER

WALL

TREAD GOES BENEATH STRINGER

NOSING BUTTS HERE

STRINGER CUT TO RECEIVE TREAD

B

Fig. 5. Stringers and treads.

same rise and run as the stair carriages, but they are cut out in reverse. The risers are butted and nailed to the riser cuts of the wall stringers, and the assembled stringers and risers are laid over the carriage. Sometimes the treads are allowed to run underneath the tread cut of the stringer. This makes it necessary to notch the tread at the nosing to fit around the stringer, as shown in Fig. 5B.

Another form of stringer is the cut-and-mitered type. This is a form of open stringer in which the ends of the risers are mitered against the vertical portion of the stringer. This construction is shown in Fig. 6 and is used when the outside stringer is to be finished and must blend with the rest of the casing or skirting board. A molding is installed on the edge of the tread and carried around to the side, making an overlap as shown in Fig. 7.

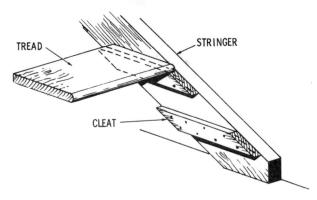

Fig. 6. Cut and mitered stringer.

BASEMENT STAIRS

Basement stairs may be built either with or without riser boards. Cutout stringers are probably the most widely used support for the treads, but the tread may be fastened to the stringers by cleats, as shown in Fig. 8. Fig. 9 shows two methods of terminating basement stairs at the floor line.

NEWELS AND HANDRAILS

All stairways should have a handrail from floor to floor. For closed stairways, the rail is attached to the wall with suitable

114

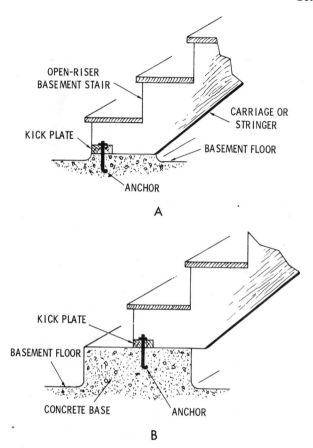

OPEN-RISER
BASEMENT STAIR

CARRIAGE OR
STRINGER

KICK PLATE

BASEMENT FLOOR

ANCHOR

A

KICK PLATE

BASEMENT FLOOR

CONCRETE BASE

ANCHOR

B

Fig. 7. The use of molding on the edge of treads.

metal brackets. The rails should be set 2′ 8″ above the tread at the riser line. Handrails and balusters are used for open stairs and for open spaces around stairs. The handrail ends against the newel post, as shown in Fig. 10.

Stairs should be laid out so that stock parts may be used for newels, rails, balusters, goosenecks, and turnouts. These parts are a matter of design and appearance, so they may be very plain or elaborate, but they should be in keeping with the style of the house. The balusters are doweled or dovetailed into the

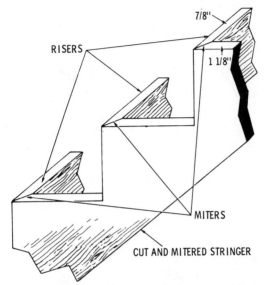

7/8"

RISERS

1 1/8"

MITERS

CUT AND MITERED STRINGER

Fig. 8. Showing the cleats stringer used in basement stairs.

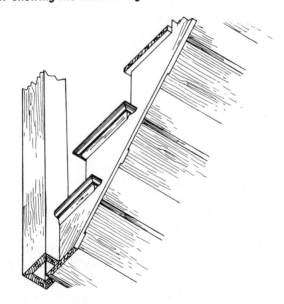

Fig. 9. Basement stair termination at floor line.

treads and, in some cases, are covered by a return nosing. Newel posts should be firmly anchored, and where half-newels are attached to a wall, blocking should be provided at the time the wall is framed.

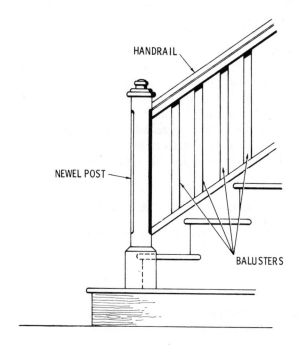

Fig. 10. Illustrating the newel post, balusters, and handrail.

DISAPPEARING STAIRS

Where attics are used primarily for storage, and where space for a fixed stairway is not available, hinged or disappearing stairs are often used. Such stairways may be purchased ready to install. They operate through an opening in the ceiling of a hall and swing up into the attic space, out of the way when not in use. Where such stairs are to be provided, the attic floor should be designed for regular floor loading.

117

EXTERIOR STAIRS

Proportioning of risers and treads in laying out porch steps or approaches to terraces should be as carefully considered as the design of interior stairways. Similar riser-to-tread ratios can be used, however. The riser used in principal exterior steps should be between 6 and 7 inches. The need for a good support or foundation for outside steps is often overlooked. Where wood steps are used, the bottom step should be set in concrete. Where the steps are located over back fill or disturbed ground, the foundation should be carried down to undisturbed ground. Fig. 11 shows the foundation and details of the step treads, handrail, and stringer, and the method of installing them. This type of step is most common in field construction and outside porch steps. The material generally used for this type of stair construction is 2 × 4s and 2 × 6s.

GLOSSARY OF STAIR TERMS

The terms generally used in stair design may be defined as follows:

Balusters—The vertical members supporting the handrail on open stairs (Fig. 12).

Carriage—The rough timber supporting the treads and risers of wood stairs, sometimes referred to as the string or stringer, as shown in Fig. 13.

Circular Stairs—A staircase with steps planned in a circle, all the steps being winders (Fig. 14).

Flight of Stairs—The series of steps leading from one landing to another.

Front String or Stringer—The stringer on that side of the stairs over which the handrail is placed.

Fillet—A band nailed to the face of a front string below the curve and extending the width of a tread.

Flyers—Steps in a flight of stairs parallel to each other.

Half-Space—The interval between two flights of steps in a staircase.

Handrail—The top finishing piece on the railing intended to be grasped by the hand in ascending and descending. For

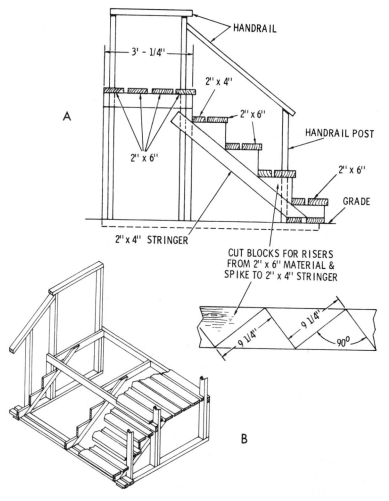

Fig. 11. Outside step construction.

closed stairs where there is no railing, the handrail is attached to the wall with brackets. Various forms of handrails are shown in Fig. 15.

Housing—The notches in the string board of a stair for the reception of steps.

Landing—The floor at the top or bottom of each story where the flight ends or begins.

119

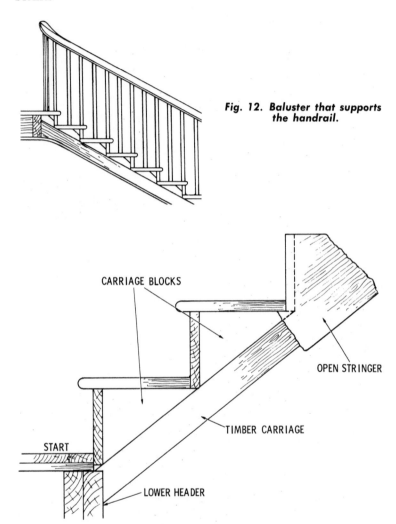

Fig. 12. Baluster that supports the handrail.

Fig. 13. Carriage blocks connected to a stair stringer.

Newel—The main post of the railing at the start of the stairs and the stiffening posts at the angles and platform.

Nosing—The projection of tread beyond the face of the riser (Fig. 16).

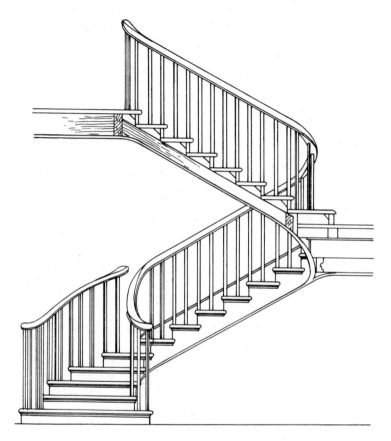

Fig. 14. A typical circular staircase.

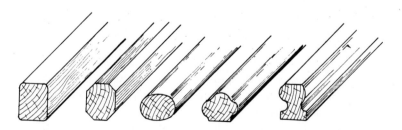

Fig. 15. Various forms of handrails.

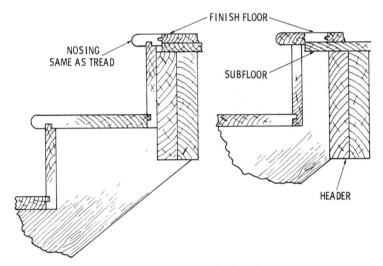

Fig. 16. The nosing installed to the tread.

Rise—The vertical distance between the treads or for the entire stairs.

Riser—The board forming the vertical portion of the front of the step, as shown in Fig. 17.

Run—The total length of stairs including the platform.

Stairs—The steps used to ascend and descend from one story to another.

Staircase—The whole set of stairs with the side members supporting the steps.

Straight Flight of Stairs—One having the steps parallel and at right angles to the strings.

String or Stringer—One of the inclined sides of a stair supporting the tread and riser. Also, a similar member, whether a support or not, such as finish stock placed exterior to the carriage on open stairs, and next to the walls on closed stairs, to give finish to the staircase. *Open stringers,* both rough and finish stock, are cut to follow the lines of the treads and risers. *Closed stringers* have parallel sides, with the risers and treads being housed into them (Fig. 18).

Tread—The horizontal face of a step, as shown in Fig. 17.

Winders—The radiating or wedge-shaped treads at the turn of a stairway.

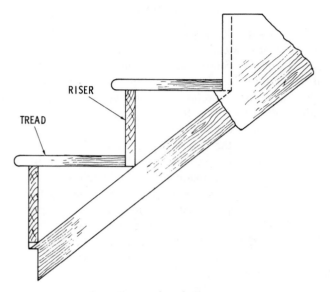

Fig. 17. Tread and riser.

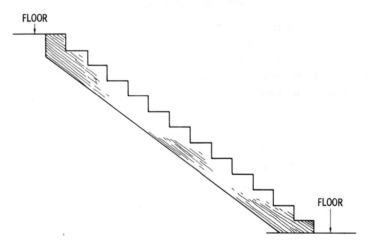

Fig. 18. The stair stringer.

123

SUMMARY

Stairways should always be designed, arranged, and installed so as to afford safety, adequate headroom, and space for passage of furniture. Stairs may be built in place, or they may be built as a complete unit in the shop and set in place.

There is a definite relationship between the height of a riser and the width of a tread. If the steps are too short, the foot may hit the leg riser at each step and an attempt to shorten the stride may be tiring. As the height of the riser is increased, the width of the tread must be decreased for comfortable results.

When openings are made in a floor, such as for a stairwell, headers and trimmer joists must be used to strengthen the floor around the opening. Stringers, which are the supports for the tread and riser, are installed between floor levels. There are several forms of stringers classed according to the method of attaching the risers and treads. The different types are cleated, cut, built-up, and rabbeted.

REVIEW QUESTIONS

1. What are stringers, risers, and treads?
2. Name the four types of stringers.
3. When is a center or third stringer used?
4. How is the rise figured when designing a stairway?
5. What is the carriage of a stairs?

CHAPTER 8

Flooring

After the foundation, sills, and floor joists have been constructed, the subfloor is laid diagonally on the joists. The floor joist forms a framework for the subfloor. This floor is called the rough floor, or subfloor, and may be viewed as a large platform covering the entire width and length of the building. Two layers or coverings of flooring material (subflooring and finished flooring) are placed on the joists. You may use 1 × 4 boards or 1 × 6 tongue-and-groove sheathing or $1/2$ plywood for the subfloor. Plywood is fastest, but usually costs the most. Fig. 1 shows the method of laying a subfloor.

It may be laid before or after the walls are framed, but preferably before, so that it can be used as a floor to work on while framing the walls. The subflooring will also give protection against the weather for tools and material stored in the basement.

INSTALLING SUBFLOORING

Tongue-and-groove boards should be installed so that each board will bear on at least two joists, and so there will be no two adjoining boards with end joints occurring between the same pair of joists. Subflooring is nailed to each joist with two eightpenny nails for widths under 8 inches and with three nails for over 8-inch widths. The subflooring may be applied either diagonally or at right angles to the joists. When the subfloor is placed at right angles to the joists, the finish floor should be laid at right angles to the subflooring. Diagonal subflooring permits

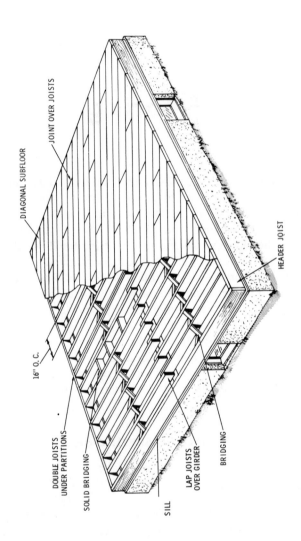

JOINT OVER JOISTS

DIAGONAL SUBFLOOR

HEADER JOIST

16" O. C.

DOUBLE JOISTS
UNDER PARTITIONS

SOLID BRIDGING

SILL

LAP JOISTS
OVER GIRDER

BRIDGING

‡Wood strip flooring, 25/32 inch thick or less, may be installed in either direction.

Fig. 1. Typical subflooring.

the finish floor to be laid either parallel or perpendicular to the joists.

The joist spacing should not exceed 16 inches on center when finish flooring is laid parallel to the joists or when parquet finish flooring is used. Indeed, it is good to check with local building codes for requirements. Where balloon framing is used, blocking should be installed between the ends of the joists at the wall for nailing the ends of diagonal subfloor boards. In areas where rain may occur during construction, square-edge boards should be laid with open joints for drainage. Tongue-and-groove boards should have holes drilled at suitable intervals to allow runoff of rain water.

Table 1 shows the thickness of the plywood and joist spacings as suggested by the Federal Housing Administration for plywood subfloor when used as a base for wood finish floors, resilient flooring, and ceramic tile.

When used as a base for parquet wood finish flooring less than $^{25}/_{32}$ inch thick, or resilient flooring, or ceramic tile, install solid blocking under all edges at right angles to the floor joists. Nail securely to the joists and blocking with nails 6 inches on center

Table 1. Plywood Thickness and Joists Spacing

Minimum thickness of five-ply subfloor	Medium thickness of finish flooring	Maximum joist spacing
†½ inch	25/32 inch wood laid at right angles to joists	24 inches
†½ inch	25/32 inch wood laid parallel to joists	20 inches
½ inch	25/32 inch wood laid at right angles to joists	20 inches
½ inch	Less than 25/32 inch wood or other finish	‡16 inches
†⅝ inch	Less than 25/32 inch wood or other finish	‡20 inches
†¾ inch	Less than 25/32 inch wood or other finish	‡24 inches

† Installed with outer plies of subflooring at right angles to joists.
‡ Wood strip flooring, 25/32 inch thick or less, may be applied in either direction.

at the intermediate framing members. When used for leveling purposes over other subflooring, the minimum thickness is $1/4$-inch three-ply.

FLOOR COVERINGS

There is a wide variety of finish flooring available, each having properties suited to a particular usage. Of these properties, durability and ease of cleaning are essential in all cases. Specific service requirements may call for special properties, such as resistance to hard wear in storehouses and on loading platforms; comfort to users in offices and shops; and attractive appearance, which is always desirable in residences.

Both hardwoods and softwoods are available as strip flooring in a variety of widths and thicknesses, as well as random-width planks, parquetry, and block flooring. Other materials include those mentioned above. A detailed roundup follows.

Wood Strip Flooring

Softwoods most commonly used for flooring are southern yellow pine, Douglas fir, redwood, western larch, and western hemlock. It is customary to divide the softwoods into two classes:

1. Vertical or edge grain.
2. Flat grain.

Each class is separated into select and common grades. The select grades designated as "B and better" grades, and sometimes the "C" grade, are used when the purpose is to stain, varnish, or wax the floor. The "C" grade is well suited for floors to be stained dark or painted, and lower grades are for rough usage when covered with carpeting. Softwood flooring is manufactured in several widths. In some places, the $2^1/2$-inch width is preferred, while in others the $3^1/2$-inch width is more popular. Softwood flooring has tongue-and-groove edges and may be hollow backed or grooved. Vertical-grain flooring stands up better than flat-grain under hard usage.

Hardwoods most commonly used for flooring are red and white oak, hard maple, beech, and birch. Maple, beech, and birch come in several grades, such as *first, second,* and *third.* Other hardwoods that are manufactured into flooring, although not commonly used, are walnut, cherry, ash, hickory, pecan, sweetgum, and sycamore. Hardwood flooring is manufactured in a variety of widths and thicknesses, some of which are referred to as standard patterns, others as special patterns. The widely used standard patterns consist of relatively narrow strips laid lengthwise in a room, as shown in Fig. 2. The most widely used standard pattern is $^{25}/_{32}$ inch thick and has a face width of $2^1/_4$ inches. One edge has a tongue and the other end has a groove, and the ends are similarly matched. The strips are random lengths, varying from 1 to 16 feet in length. The number of short pieces will depend on the grade used. Similar patterns of flooring are available in thicknesses of $^{15}/_{32}$ and $^{11}/_{32}$ inch, with a face width of $1^1/_2$ inches, and with square edges and a flat back.

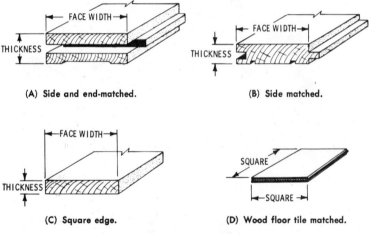

(A) Side and end-matched.

(B) Side matched.

(C) Square edge.

(D) Wood floor tile matched.

Fig. 2. Types of finished hardwood flooring.

The flooring is generally hollow backed. The top face is slightly wider than the bottom, so that the strips are driven tight together at the top side but the bottom edges are slightly open. The tongue should fit snugly in the groove to eliminate squeaks in the floor.

Another pattern of flooring used to a limited degree is $^3/_8$ inch thick with a face width of $1^1/_2$ and 2 inches, with square edges and a flat back. Fig. 2D shows a type of wood floor tile commonly known as parquetry.

INSTALLATION OF WOOD STRIP FLOORING

Flooring should be laid after the wall and ceiling are completed, after windows and exterior doors are in place, and after most of the interior trim is installed. The subfloor should be clean and level, and should be covered with a 15-lb. asphalt building paper, as shown in Fig. 3. This building paper will stop a certain amount of dust and will somewhat deaden the sound. Where a crawl space is used, it will increase the warmth of the floor by preventing air infiltration. The location of the joists should be chalklined on the paper as a guide for nailing.

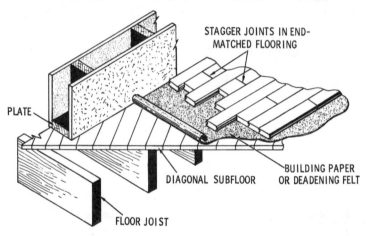

Fig. 3. Installation of strip flooring showing the use of deadening felt or heavy building paper.

Strip flooring should be laid crosswise of the floor joists, and it looks best when the floor is laid lengthwise in a rectangular room. Since joists generally span the short way in a living room, that room establishes the direction for flooring in other rooms. Flooring should be delivered only during dry weather and should be stored in the warmest and driest place available in the house. The recommended average moisture content for flooring at the time of installation should be between 6 and 10 percent. Moisture absorbed after the material is delivered to the house site is one of the most common causes of open joints between floor strips. It will show up several months after the floor has been laid.

Floor squeaks are caused by the movement of one board against another. Such movement may occur because the floor joists are too light and are not held down tightly, tongue fitting too loose in the grooves, or because of poor nailing. Adequate nailing is one of the most important means of minimizing squeaks. When it is possible to nail the finish floor through the subfloor into the joist, a much better job is obtained than if the finish floor is nailed only to the subfloor. Various types of nails are used in nailing various thicknesses of flooring. For $^{25}/_{32}$-inch flooring, it is best to use eightpenny steel cut flooring nails; for $^{1}/_{2}$-inch flooring, sixpenny nails should be used. Other types of nails have been developed in recent years for nailing of flooring, among these being the annularly grooved and spirally grooved nails. In using these nails, it is well to check with the floor manufacturer's recommendation as to size and diameter for a specific use. Fig. 4 shows the method of nailing the first strip of flooring. The nail is driven straight down through the board at the groove

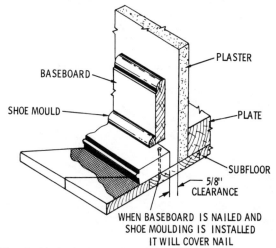

Fig. 4. Method of laying the first strips of wood flooring.

edge. The nails should be driven into the joist and near enough to the edge so that they will be covered by the base or shoe molding. The first strip of flooring can be nailed through the tongue.

Fig. 5 shows the nail driven in at an angle of between 45° and 50° where the tongue adjoins the shoulder. Do not try to drive the nail down with a hammer, as the wood may be easily struck and damaged. Instead use a nail set to finish off the driving. Fig. 6 shows the position of the nail set commonly used for the final driving. In order to avoid splitting the wood, it is sometimes necessary to pre-drill the holes through the tongue. This will also help to drive the nail easily into the joist. For the second course of flooring, select a piece so that the butt joints will be well separated from those in the first course. For floors to be covered with rugs, the long lengths could be used at the sides of the room and the short lengths in the center where they will be covered.

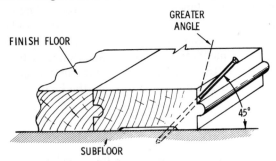

Fig. 5. Nailing method for strip wood flooring.

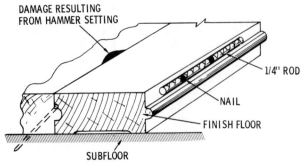

Fig. 6. Suggested method for setting nails in flooring.

Each board should be driven up tightly, but do not strike the tongue with the hammer, as this may crush the wood. Use a piece of scrap flooring for a driving block. Crooked pieces may require wedging to force them into alignment. This is necessary in order that the last piece of flooring will be parallel to the baseboard. If the room is not square, it may be necessary to start the alignment at an early stage.

SOUNDPROOF FLOORS

One of the most effective sound-resistant floors is called a *floating* floor. The upper or finish floor is constructed on 2 × 2 joists actually floating on glass wool mats, as shown in Fig. 7. There should be absolutely no mechanical connection through the glass wool mat, not even a nail to either the subfloor or the wall.

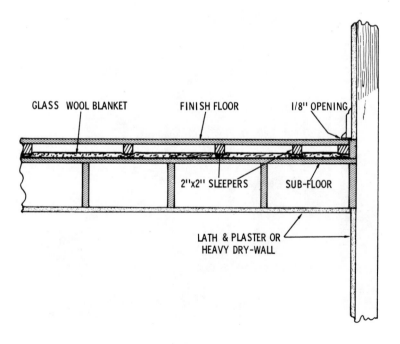

Fig. 7. A sound-resistant floor.

WOOD-TILE FLOORING

Flooring manufacturers have developed a wide variety of special patterns of flooring, including parquet, which is nailed in place or has an adhesive backing (Fig. 8), that can be used over wood subfloors or concrete slabs. One common type of floor tile is a block 9 inches square and $13/16$ inch thick that is made up of several individual strips of flooring held together with glue and splines. Two edges have a tongue and the opposite edges are grooved. Numerous other sizes and thicknesses are available. In laying the floor, the direction of the blocks is alternated to create a checkerboard effect. The manufacturer supplies instructions for laying their tile, and it is advisable to follow them carefully. When the tiles are used over a concrete slab, a vapor barrier

Fig. 8. Parquet tiles are real wood with adhesive backing. Courtesy of United Gilsonite.

should be used. The slab should be level, and should be thoroughly cured and dry before the wood tile is laid.

CERAMIC TILE

Ceramic tile (Fig. 9) is made in different colors and with both glazed and unglazed surfaces. It is used as a covering for floors in bathrooms, entryways, kitchens, and fireplace hearths. Ceramic tile presents a hard and impervious surface. In addition to standard sizes and plain colors, many tiles are especially made to carry out architectural effects. When ceramic-tile floors are used with wood-frame construction, a concrete bed of adequate thickness must be installed to receive the finishing layer.

Installation of tile is done with adhesive. Check with your dealer for specific instructions.

Fig. 9. Ceramic tile. It has moved out of the bathroom. **Courtesy of Olean Tile.**

OTHER FINISHED FLOORINGS

The carpenter and do-it-yourselfer can select from a wealth of floor coverings. Perhaps the chief development has been resilient flooring, so-called because it "gives" when you step on it. There are 12-inch tiles available for installing with adhesive, as well as adhesive-backed tiles. Today most tile is vinyl and comes in a tremendous variety of styles, colors, and patterns. The newest in flooring is the so-called waxless flooring, which requires renewal with a waxlike material after a certain period of time.

Fig. 10. Resilient flooring is first laid in a room.

Resilient flooring also comes in sheets or rolls 12 feet wide. It, too, is chiefly vinyl and comes in a great array of styles and colors. It is more difficult to install than tile (Figs. 10–14).

Resilient sheet flooring comes in several qualities, and you should check competing materials before you buy. Vinyl resilient flooring may be installed anywhere in the house, above or below grade, with no worry about moisture problems. An adequate subfloor, usually of particleboard or plywood, is required.

Fig. 11. Relief cuts are made where flooring abuts walls. Courtesy of Congoleum.

Fig. 12. A utility knife is used to trim flooring. Courtesy of Congoleum.

137

Also available is carpeting. Wall-to-wall carpet installation is a professional job, but carpet tiles can be had. They are available for indoor and outdoor use and are popularly used in kitchens and bathrooms.

Other flooring materials include paint-on coatings and paints. Paint is normally used in areas where economy is most important.

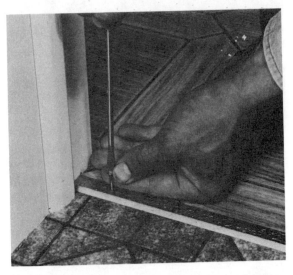

Fig. 13. Metal threshold is screwed in place. Courtesy of Congoleum.

SUMMARY

After the foundation, sills, and floor joists have been constructed, the subfloor is laid. Boards or plywood are used.

Hardwood floorings most commonly used are red and white oak, hard maple, beech, and birch. Most flooring is $^{25}/_{32}$ inch thick with a face width of $2^{1}/_{4}$ inches. The finished flooring is usually installed after all plastering is complete, after windows and doors are in place, and after most of the interior trim has been installed.

When the flooring is ready for installation, the subfloor should be thoroughly cleaned. A layer of deadening felt or building

Fig. 14. The final step is to reinstall molding. Courtesy of Congoleum.

paper will stop a certain amount of dust and will somewhat deaden the sound, plus it will help to eliminate floor squeaks. Where a crawl space is used, it will increase the warmth of the floor by preventing air infiltration.

REVIEW QUESTIONS

1. What type of wood is generally used for finish flooring?
2. What is the thickness of hardwood flooring?
3. Why is building paper or deadening felt used between flooring?
4. How are soundproof floors constructed?
5. Why is subflooring generally installed diagonally to floor joists?

CHAPTER 9

Interior Walls and Ceilings

Far and away the most common material for building interior walls and ceilings is drywall, variously known as gypsum board, plasterboard, and Sheetrock (a brand name). It is estimated that 80 percent of new homes utilize drywall for walls and ceilings. The reasons are simple. It is easier to install than plaster—much easier—and it goes up much faster.

Plaster, also known as wetwall, is still used in certain parts of the country, but not nearly so often as formerly. It takes a good deal of skill to apply plaster correctly, and it is both time- and labor-consuming. On the other hand, it is generally conceded that a plaster wall is better than plasterboard in a couple of ways, especially sound transmission and smoothness.

Whatever he uses, it is important for the craftsman to know how both drywall and plaster walls and ceilings are built. The chances are good that carpenters and others will be involved only with plasterboard, but the anatomy of a plaster wall and ceiling is important to know simply because it has been used in many homes, and a craftsman should know the anatomy of the complete house.

PLASTER

When plaster is used to form the wall surface, it is held in place by lath. There are several kinds of lath, classed according to material:

1. Expanded metal.
2. Gypsum.

141

PLASTER REINFORCING

Since some drying may take place in wood framing members after the house is completed, some shrinkage can be expected. This, in turn, may cause the plaster to crack around openings and corners. To minimize this cracking, expanded metal lath is used in certain key positions over the plaster base material as reinforcement. Strips of expanded metal lath may be used over the window and door openings, as shown in Fig. 1. A strip 8″ × 20″, placed diagonally across each upper corner and nailed lightly in place, should be effective. Fig. 2 illustrates a number of types of expanded metal lath.

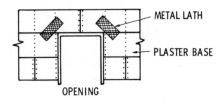

Fig. 1. Reinforcement of plaster over openings using expanded metal lath.

Inside corners at the juncture of walls and ceilings should be reinforced with corners of metal lath or wire fabric, as shown in Fig. 3, except where special clip systems are used for installing the lath. The minimum width of the lath in the corners should be 5 inches, or 2½ inches on each surface or internal angle, and should also be lightly nailed in place. Corner beads, as shown in Fig. 4, of expanded metal lath or perforated metal, should be installed on all exterior corners. They should be applied plumb and level. The bead acts as a leveling edge when the walls are plastered and reinforces the corner against mechanical damage.

Metal lath should be used under large flush beams, as shown in Fig. 5, and should extend well beyond the edges. Where reinforcing is required over solid wood surfaces, such as drop beams, the metal lath should either be installed on strips or else self-furring nails should be used to set the lath out from the beam. The lath should be lapped on all adjoining gypsum lath surfaces.

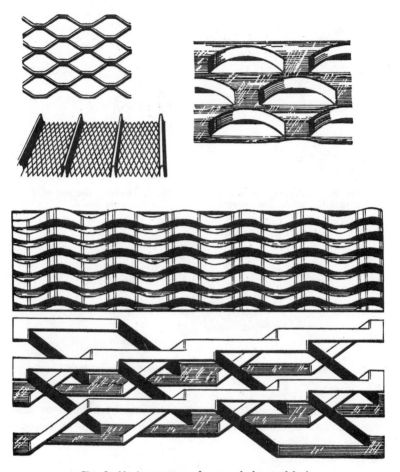

Fig. 2. Various types of expanded metal lath.

Expanded metal lath applied around a bathtub recess for ceramic tile application should be used over a paper backing, as shown in Fig. 6. Studs should be covered with 15-pound asphalt saturated felt applied shingle style. The scratch coat should be Portland-cement plaster, $5/8$-inch minimum thickness, and integrally waterproofed. The scratch coat should be dry before the ceramic tile is applied. Expanded metal lath consists of sheet metal that has been slit and expanded to form innumerable open-

143

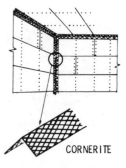

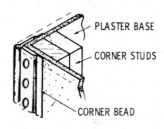

Fig. 3. Illustrating the use of
cornerites made from metal
lath.

Fig. 4. Showing the use of a
corner bead.

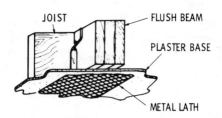

Fig. 5. Illustrating the use of expanded metal lath
under large flush beams.

ings for the keying of the plaster. It should be painted or galvanized, and its minimum weights for 16-inch stud or joist spacing are as follows:

Use	Pounds per square yard
Walls	2.5
Ceilings	3.4
Ceiling with flat rib	2.75

Metal lath is usually $27'' \times 96''$ in size. Other materials, such as
wood lath, woven wire fabric, and galvanized wire fabric, may
also be used as a plaster base. Various types of woven wire lath
are shown in Fig. 7.

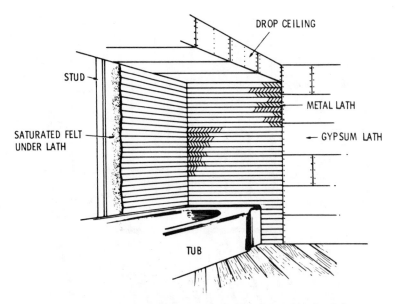

Fig. 6. Application of expanded metal lath around bathtub for the installation of ceramic tile.

INSTALLING GYPSUM BASE

A plaster finish requires a base on which the plaster can be spread. The base must have bonding qualities so that the plaster adheres or is keyed to the base that has been fastened to the framing members. One of the popular types of plaster base that may be used on the side walls and ceilings is gypsum-board lath. Such lath is generally 16″ × 48″ and is applied horizontally (across) the frame members. This type of board has a paper face with a gypsum filler. For studs and joists with spacing of 16 inches on center, 3/8-inch thickness is used, and for 24 inches on center spacing, 1/2-inch thickness is used. This material can be obtained with a foil backing that serves as a vapor barrier, and if it faces an air space, it has some insulating value. It is also available with perforations, which improves the bonding strength of the plaster base.

Insulating fiberboard lath may also be used as a plaster base. It is usually 1/2-inch thick and generally comes in strips of 18″ ×

145

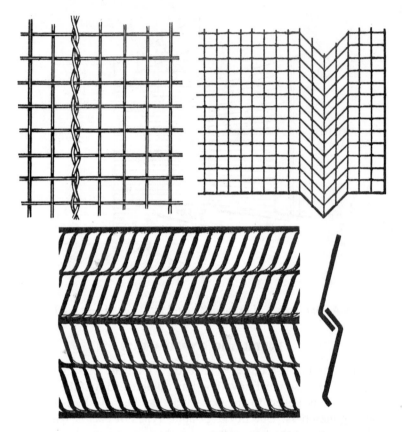

Fig. 7. Various types of woven wire lath.

48″. It often has a shiplap edge and may be used with metal clips that are located between studs or joists to stiffen the horizontal joints. Fiberboard lath has a value as insulation and may be used on the walls or ceilings adjoining exterior or unheated areas.

Gypsum lath should be applied horizontally, with the joints broken as shown in Fig. 8. Vertical joints should be made over the center of the studs or joists, and should be nailed with 13-gauge gypsum lathing nails $1\frac{1}{8}$ inches long and having a $\frac{3}{8}$-inch flat head. Nails should be spaced 4 inches on center and should be nailed at each stud or joist crossing. Lath joints over the heads of door and window openings should not occur at the jamb lines. Insulating lath should be installed much like gypsum lath, except that 13-gauge $1^{1}/_{4}$-inch blued nails should be used.

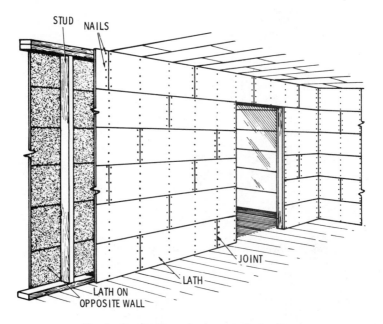

Fig. 8. Application of gypsum plaster base.

PLASTER GROUNDS

Plaster grounds are strips of wood the same thickness as the lath and plaster, and are attached to the framing before the plaster is applied. Plaster grounds are used around window and door openings as a plaster stop, and along the floor line for attaching the baseboard. They also serve as a leveling surface when plastering, and as a nailing base for the finish trim, as shown in Fig. 9. There are two types of plaster grounds: those that remain in place (Fig. 10), and those that are removed after plastering is completed (Fig. 11). The grounds that remain in place are usually $^{7}/_{8}$-inch thick and may vary in width from 1 inch around openings to 2 inches for those used along the floor line. These

147

grounds are nailed securely in place before the plaster base is installed. Where a painted finish is used, finished door jambs are sometimes placed in the rough openings, and the edges of the jambs serve as the grounds during operation.

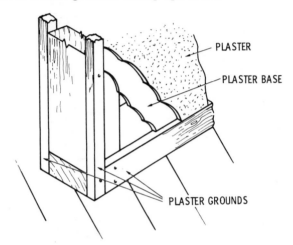

PLASTER

PLASTER BASE

PLASTER GROUNDS

Fig. 9. Plaster grounds used at doors and floor line.

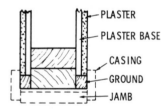

PLASTER

PLASTER BASE

CASING

GROUND

JAMB

Fig. 10. Illustrating plaster grounds that stay in place and are used as a nailing base for the trim.

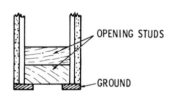

OPENING STUDS

GROUND

Fig. 11. Showing the plaster grounds that are removed after plastering.

NAILING LATH

Lath nailers are horizontal or vertical members to which lath, gypsum boards, or other covering materials are nailed. These members are required at interior corners of the walls and at the juncture of the wall and ceiling. Vertical lath nailers may be composed of studs so arranged as to provide nailing surfaces, as shown in Fig. 12. This construction also provides a good tie between walls.

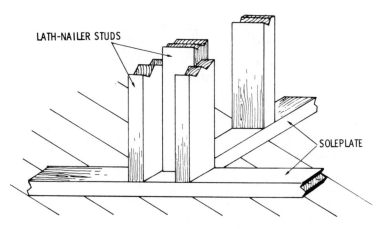

LATH-NAILER STUDS

SOLEPLATE

Fig. 12. Lath nailers at wall intersections.

Another vertical nailer construction consists of a 2″ × 6″ lathing board that is nailed to the stud of the intersecting wall, as shown in Fig. 13. Lathing headers are used to back up the board. The header should be toenailed to the stud. Doubling of the ceiling joist over the wallplates provides a nailing surface for interior finish material, as shown in Fig. 14. Walls may be tied to the ceiling framing in this method by toenailing through the joists into the wall plates.

Another method of providing nailing surface at the ceiling line is similar to that used on the walls. A 1″ × 6″ lathing board is nailed to the wall plate as shown in Fig. 15. Headers are used to back up this board, and the header, in turn, can be tied to the wall by toenailing into the wall plate.

PLASTERING MATERIAL AND METHOD OF APPLICATION

Plaster for interior finishing is made from combinations of sand, lime or prepared plaster, and water. Waterproof finish wall materials are available and should be used in bathrooms, especially in showers or tub recesses when tile is not used, and sometimes in the kitchen wainscot. Plaster should be applied in

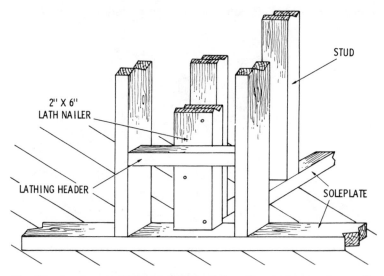

Fig. 13. Another method of installing lath nailers at intersection walls.

STUD

2" X 6"
LATH NAILER

LATHING HEADER

SOLEPLATE

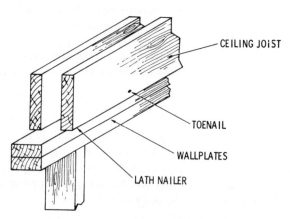

CEILING JOIST

TOENAIL

WALLPLATES

LATH NAILER

**Fig. 14. Horizontal lath nailers for plaster base
formed by ceiling joists.**

three coats or a two-coat double-up work. The minimum thickness over a lath or masonry should be $1/2$ inch. The first plaster coat over the metal lath is called the *scratch coat,* and is scratched after a slight set has occurred to ensure a good bond for the second coat. The second coat is called the *brown or level-*

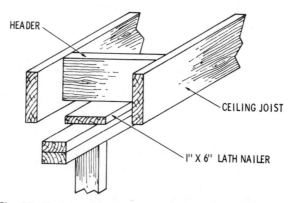

HEADER

CEILING JOIST

I" X 6" LATH NAILER

Fig. 15. Horizontal lath nailers for ceiling provided by lathing boards.

ing coat, and it is during the application of this coat that the leveling is done.

The double-up work, combining the scratch and brown coat, is used on gypsum or insulating lath, and the leveling and plumbing of walls and ceiling are done during the application of this work. The final or finish coat consists of two general types—the sand-float and the putty finish. In the sand-float finish, lime is mixed with sand and results in a textured finish, with the texture depending on the coarseness of the sand used. Putty finish is used without sand and has a smooth finish. This is commonly used in kitchens and bathrooms, where a gloss paint or enamel finish is often employed, and in other rooms where a smooth finish is desired. The plastering operation should not be done in freezing weather without the use of constant heat for protection from freezing. In normal construction, the heating unit is in place before plastering is started.

Insulating plaster, consisting of a vermiculite, perlite, or other aggregate used with the plaster mix, may also be used for wall and ceiling finishes. This aggregate properly mixed with the plaster produces small hollow air pockets, which act as insulating material. The vermiculite is a material developed from a mica base that is exploded in size, and, when mixed with the plaster, reduces the added weight in a conventional plastered wall or ceiling.

151

The following points in plaster maintenance are worthy of attention:

1. In a newly constructed house, a few small plaster cracks may develop during or after the first heating season. These cracks are usually caused by the drying and shrinking of the structural members. For this reason, it is advisable to wait until after a heating season before painting the plaster. These cracks can then be filled before painting has begun.

2. Because of the curing period ordinarily required for a plastered wall, it is not advisable to apply oil-base paints until at least 60 days after plastering is completed. Water-mix, or resin-base, paints may be applied without the necessity of an aging period.

3. Large plaster cracks often indicate a structural weakness in the framing. One of the common areas that may need correction is around a basement stairs. Framing may not be adequate for the loads of the walls and ceilings. In such cases, the use of an additional post and pedestal may be required to correct this fault. Inadequate framing around fireplaces and chimney openings, and joists that are not doubled under partitions, are other common sources of weakness.

In addition to the plastering methods described, there has been one other development in plastering that reduces the plastering process to "one coat" and that gives the process its name. Here, "green" or "blue" $5/8$-inch gypsum board is installed like regular gypsum board, and the premixed plaster material, which comes in 5-gallon cans, is applied by the plasterer. That's it. The applied material cures very hard, and the gypsum board has the tooth to keep it in place.

DRYWALL

The use of drywall board requires that the studs and ceiling joists be in alignment. Good solid rigid sheathing on the exterior walls will accomplish this on the studs, and strongback bracing on the ceiling joists (Fig. 16) will keep the ceiling joists level and in alignment.

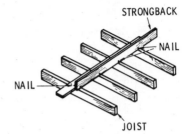

STRONGBACK

NAIL

NAIL

JOIST

Fig. 16. Strongback bracing for ceiling joists.

Gypsum board, or drywall, is a sheet material composed of a gypsum filler faced with paper. Sheets are usually 4 feet wide and can be obtained in lengths of from 8 to 12 feet. The edges along the length of the sheet are recessed to receive joint cement and tape. Although gypsum board may be used in $^3/_8$-inch thickness, a $^1/_2$-inch board offers greater resistance to deflection between framing members. Gypsum board may be applied to the walls either vertically or horizontally. Vertical applications with 4-foot-wide sheets will cover three studs when they are spaced 16 inches on center. The edges should be centered on the studs, and only moderate contact should be made between the edges of the sheet. Large-head, blued $1^5/_8$-inch drywall nails should be used with $^1/_2$-inch gypsum board, and $1^3/_8$-inch with $^3/_8$-inch board. Nails should be spaced 6 to 8 inches for side walls, and 5 to 7 inches for ceiling application, as shown in Fig. 17.

The horizontal method of application is best adapted to rooms in which full-length sheets can be used, to minimize the number of vertical joints. When joints are necessary, they should be made at windows and doors. Nail spacing is the same as that used in vertical application. Where framing members are more than 16 inches on center, solid blocking should be used along the horizontal joint, as shown in Fig. 18.

Another method of gypsum board application includes an under course of $^3/_8$-inch material applied vertically by nailing. The finish $^3/_8$-inch sheet is applied horizontally, usually in room-size lengths by means of an adhesive, with only enough nails used to hold the sheet in place until the adhesive is dry. The manufacturer's recommendations should be followed. In the finishing operation, the nails should be set about $^1/_{16}$ inch below the face of the board. This set can be obtained by using a slightly

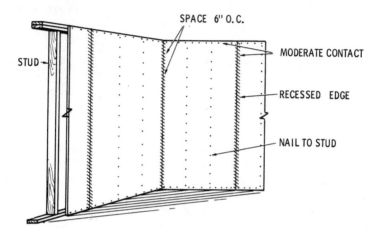

Fig. 17. Application of vertical applied drywall finish.

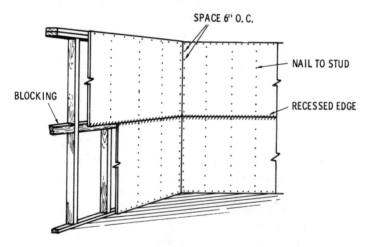

Fig. 18. Application of horizontal applied drywall finish.

crowned hammer, as shown in Fig. 19. Setting the nail in this manner, a slight dimple is formed in the face of the board without breaking the paper surface. The setting of the nail is particularly important for center nails, since the edge nailing will be covered with tape and joint cement.

Fig. 19. Nail set with crowned hammer on drywall.

**Fig. 19. Nail set with crowned
hammer on drywall.**

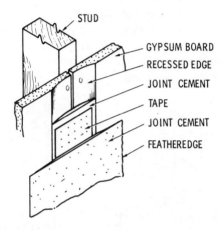

STUD

GYPSUM BOARD
RECESSED EDGE
JOINT CEMENT
TAPE
JOINT CEMENT
FEATHEREDGE

Fig. 20. Applying tape and cement to wall joints.

Joint cement is available in powder form to be mixed with water to a soft putty consistency, as well as a prepared vinyl mix. The procedure for taping joints (Fig. 20) is as follows:

1. Use a wide, broad knife (4″ to 6″) and spread the cement in the recess starting at the top of the wall.
2. Press the tape into the recess with the knife until the joint cement is forced through the perforations.
3. Cover the tape with additional cement, feathering the outer edge.
4. Allow the cement to dry and apply a second coat and feather the edges. A steel trowel is sometimes used. For best results, a third coat may be applied, feathering beyond the second coat.
5. After the joint cement has dried, sand it smooth.
6. For hiding nail indentations in the center of the board, fill with joint cement and sand smooth when dry.

Interior corners may be treated with tape. Fold the tape down the center to a right angle, as shown in Fig. 21. Apply cement to both sides and press the perforated tape into the cement. Smooth the tape down with a trowel. (There is a special corner trowel for this.) After the cement has dried, apply a second coat. Sand the cement when dry, and apply a third coat if needed. The interior corners between the wall and ceiling may be concealed by the use of a molding. When molding is used, as shown in Fig. 22, it is not necessary to tape the joints. Metal corner beads should be used on exterior corners and also for openings where a casing or trim is not used.

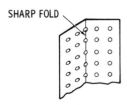

SHARP FOLD

CEILING MOLDING

Fig. 21. Folding joint tape for use on interior corners.

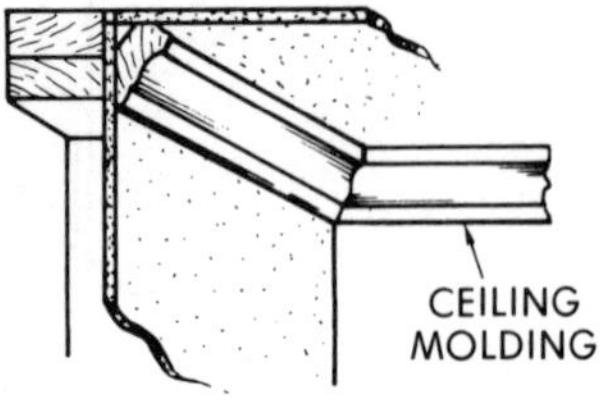

Fig. 22. Illustrating the use of molding at the wall and ceiling corner when using drywall construction.

MASONRY WALLS AS PLASTER BASE

Masonry provides an excellent base for plaster. The surface of any masonry unit should be rough to provide a good mechanical key and should be free from paint, oil, dust and dirt, or any other material that might prevent a satisfactory bond. Proper application of plaster requires:

1. That the plaster base material bonds and becomes an integral part of the base to which it is applied.
2. That it be used as a thin reinforced base for the finished surface.

Old masonry walls that have been softened by weathering, or surfaces that cannot be cleaned thoroughly, must be covered with metal reinforcement before applying the plaster. Metal reinforcement should be applied to wood furring strips, as shown in

Fig. 23. The metal reinforcement should be well braced and rigid to prevent cracking the plaster. This type of construction will give some insulating qualities due to the air space between masonry and plaster.

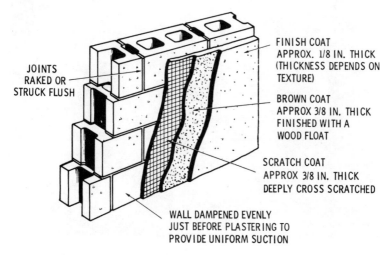

JOINTS
RAKED OR
STRUCK FLUSH

FINISH COAT
APPROX. 1/8 IN. THICK
(THICKNESS DEPENDS ON
TEXTURE)

BROWN COAT
APPROX 3/8 IN. THICK
FINISHED WITH A
WOOD FLOAT

SCRATCH COAT
APPROX 3/8 IN. THICK
DEEPLY CROSS SCRATCHED

WALL DAMPENED EVENLY
JUST BEFORE PLASTERING TO
PROVIDE UNIFORM SUCTION

Fig. 23. The application of plaster to masonry.

OTHER MATERIALS

Several other materials are available for finishing walls and ceilings. Paneling is a major material for walls; this is covered in detail in Volume 3. For ceilings, which are also touched on in the other volumes in this series, there is a good variety, as follows:

Acoustic Tiles—These come with a fissured surface in various colors and sizes, commonly from 12″ × 12″ to 2′ × 4′ and are designed to reduce sound transmission within a room (they do not keep the sound from going out of the room).

Suspended Ceiling—In Fig. 24, a metal gridwork is installed and the ceiling material, which is usually 2 × 4 panels of various colors, is dropped into the gridwork (hence its other name, *dropped ceiling*). This form of ceiling is good in basements and for covering ceilings that are in very poor shape. Also, it not

157

Fig. 24. *Suspended ceiling. You can gain access above by lifting up a panel. Courtesy of Armstrong.*

only hides paper in the basement but you can easily get at pipes by lifting out a panel from the gridwork.

Other Materials—Also available are planks (from Armstrong), which are installed on a sort of metal furring strip attached to the ceiling. It would be difficult, indeed, to determine that these planks are not actually wood (Figs. 25 and 26).

You can also get real wood strips, such as Montgomery Ward sells, for installing on ceilings (and on walls, for which they were expressly designed). There is also false brick, which is secured with adhesive, and a material that imitates stone. And there are others. A trek through the catalogue of a firm like Montgomery Ward can be enlightening.

SUMMARY

Metal lath is generally used around openings and corners to minimize cracking the plaster. Since wood draws moisture from

Fig. 25. System from Armstrong employs metal furring. Courtesy of Armstrong.

Fig. 26. Realistic imitation wood planks install easily. Courtesy of Armstrong.

the plaster, metal lath is used to reinforce the plaster. This type of material is also used to cover wide cracks and open joints in lath.

Gypsum board is another type of lath, which is usually 16″ × 48″, and is applied horizontally to the wall studs. It is obtained in $3/8$-inch and $1/2$-inch thicknesses, depending on wall stud spacing. Drywall is the most popular finish material. It is obtained in 4′ × 8′ or 4′ × 12′ sheets. The edges along the length of the sheet are recessed to receive the joint tape and cement.

REVIEW QUESTIONS

1. What are plaster grounds and why are they used?
2. Why is gypsum board or plaster board used instead of wood lath?
3. What is drywall and why is it used?
4. Why is metal lath used and where is it installed?
5. What is joint tape and how is it used?

CHAPTER 10

Table Saws

The table saw is one of the most popular tools in any wood-working shop or plant. Plants usually have one or more power saws used exclusively for ripping and one or more for crosscutting. The table saw can do both. Beveling and mitering can also be done with table saws, while grooving and dadoing can also be done by means of special cutters.

In use, the stock is fed along the table and across the saw, from which the revolving blade just projects (Fig. 1). If you wish, you can tilt the blade for making angled or beveled cuts (Fig. 2), and the tool can also be equipped with accessories such as the dado head, with which you can make rabbet cuts and grooves.

CONSTRUCTION

The tool, Fig. 2, generally consists of an iron base or frame on which a table is mounted and an arbor or shaft that carries the saw blade or other cutter. The arbor or shaft revolves in two bearings, which are bolted to the frame. It is driven by a belt that passes over a pulley; this pulley is fastened to the shaft between two bearings.

When wood is cut on a table saw, it must be firmly held against a metal guide or fence, which can be set at any convenient distance from the saw blade. When the fence is used as a guide for cutting boards lengthwise, the operation is known as *ripping*. Table saws are equipped with slots or grooves to accommodate a miter gauge, which is used as a guide when sawing across a board; this operation is known as *crosscutting*.

Fig. 1. When cutting, table saw blade should barely project from stock. Courtesy of the American Plywood Assn.

RIPPING OPERATION

One of the most useful operations of the table saw is that of ripping stock to its required width, as shown in Figs. 3 to 5. This operation is generally accomplished as follows:

1. The fence is set to the graduated scale at the front of the table to cut the required width.
2. The saw is adjusted (raised or lowered) to project approximately 1/4 inch above the stock to be ripped.
3. The splitter and saw guard are positioned to ensure safe operation.
4. The operation is started by holding the work close to the fence and pushing it toward the rotating saw blade with a

162

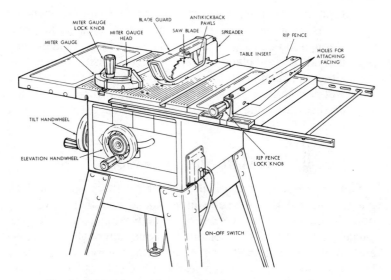

Fig. 2. Parts of a table saw, also known as a bench saw.

ALWAYS SUPPORT LONG WORKPIECES

Fig. 3. It's best to support long stock before ripping.

firm, even motion. A smooth, uniform speed of feed should be used; avoid jerky movements and jamming the work through too quickly. The operator should not stand directly behind the saw blade but should take a position slightly to either side and hold the stock near its end so that one hand will pass to the right and the other hand will pass to the left of the saw blade. A short stick is used to push narrow pieces of stock through.

CROSSCUTTING OPERATION

Square crosscutting work on the table saw is performed by placing the work against the miter gauge and then advancing both the gauge and the work toward the rotating saw blade. The gauge may be used in either table groove, although most operators prefer the left-hand groove for average work. It is essential that the miter gauge is set correctly in order to obtain a square cut; therefore, it is customary to test the work by means of a try square before proceeding.

MITERING OPERATIONS

Most miters are cut to an angle of 45° because four pieces cut at this angle will make a square or a rectangle when assembled. Miters are cut by setting the miter gauge at the required number of degrees. The angle of the miter for any regular polygon is obtained by dividing 180° by the number of sides and subtracting the quotient from 90°. For example, to find the angle for the miter of a pentagon (5 sides), we have $90 - (180/5) = 54°$. Similarly, the angle for the miter of an octagon (8 sides) will be $90 - (180/8) = 67.5°$. The miter gauge may be used in either of the table grooves and also may be set on either side of the center position. When great accuracy is required on miter cuts, special miter-clamp attachments are used.

GROOVING OPERATIONS

These operations consist of making grooves that are wider than those cut by ordinary saw blades. Grooves of varying

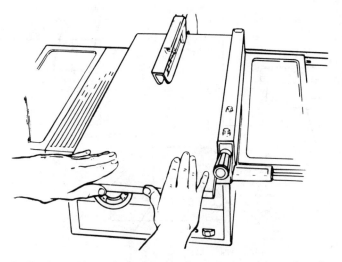

Fig. 4. Ripping wide stock on the saw. Fence is set so that edge of stock rides against it.

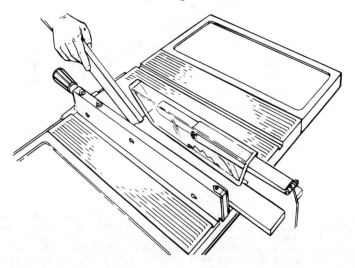

Fig. 5. For safety it's best to use a push stick when stock is narrow.

widths are commonly cut on a table saw by employing a special attachment known as a *dado head*. This "head" is made up of two outside cutters and three or four inside cutters, as shown in

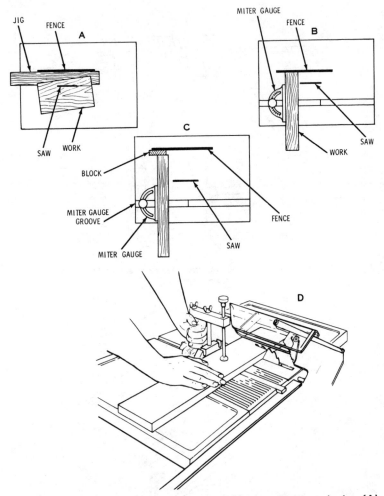

Fig. 6. Typical sawing operations on the table saw. In taper ripping (A), work that is to be ripped on a taper cannot be guided against the fence but must be held in a tapering jig. The same idea can be applied to a number of other forms. When cutting shoulders, the stock should first be squared on one end and cut to the desired length. The miter gauge is used in conjunction with the fence to bring the shoulder cut the correct distance from the end (B). When crosscutting wide pieces to length, one end should first be squared and the gauge adjusted to the required length. Narrow pieces may be sawed to length by placing a block against the fence (C); the distance from the saw blade to the block is then the required length. Note the hold-down device (D) when making a crosscut bevel cut.

Fig. 7, by means of which grooves varying in width of from $1/8$ to $13/16$ inch or larger can be made by using different combinations of cutters. The outside cutters generally have eight sections of cutting teeth and four raker teeth. The eight sections of cutting teeth are ground alternately left and right to divide the cut. Inside cutters of $1/8$ inch and $1/4$ inch are usually swage set for clearance.

Fig. 7. A typical dado-head assembly. A dado head, as shown, is made up of two outside blades $1/8$ inch thick together with one or more cutting fillers $1/16$ inch and $1/8$ inch thick, depending on the width of the groove desired. Grooves varying in widths up to 1 inch can be cut.

Grooves which are cut across the grain are termed *dadoes*. They are usually cut at right angles, but may also be cut at other angles. Dadoes that do not extend entirely from one side of a board to the other side are called *stopped dadoes, blind dadoes,* or *gains*. A gain may have one open end, or both ends may be closed. Two grooving operations are shown in Figs. 8 and 9.

SUMMARY

The efficiency of a table saw depends mainly on the type and condition of the blade used. There are generally three types of table-saw blades: crosscut, ripsaw, and combination.

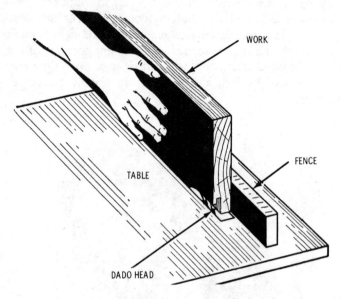

Fig. 8. The method of cutting a rabbeted joint with a dado head. Joints of this type are used extensively in drawer construction.

Fig. 9. The method of cutting wide grooves with a dado head.

Many operations can be performed on a table saw, such as ripping, rabbeting, dado cutting, miter cutting, molding cutting, and cutting tenons. In the conventional design, the saw can be tilted to an angle of 45 degrees, which is a safety factor since the operator does not have to work in an awkward position. When wood is cut on a table saw, it must be firmly held against a metal guide or fence.

REVIEW QUESTIONS

1. Why is it better to tilt the saw blade than to tilt the table in miter cuts?
2. Explain the purpose of the fence.
3. What is a dado head?
4. What is rabbeting?

CHAPTER 11

Band Saws

Band saws are manufactured for many uses. For industrial ripping and resawing, large machines with blades from 3 to 5 inches wide are generally used. The type most adaptable to the general wood shop has blades from $1/2$ to 1 inch wide and is used particularly for cutting curved outlines.

Essentially, a band saw consists of a table, wheels, guides, saw blade, and suitable guards. The average table can be tilted, usually 45° in one direction and 10° in the other. Some, however, are built to permit bevel cutting by varying the blade angle. The band saw is generally used for resawing because of its thinner kerf.

ANATOMY

A band saw, Fig. 1, such as is used in woodworking shops, consists generally of an endless band of steel with saw teeth on one edge, passing over two vertical wheels and through a slot in a table. The blade is held in position by a guide.

The two vertical wheels over which the blade is fitted are usually made of cast iron; their rims are equipped with rubber linings and are provided with adjustments for centering the saw on the rims and for giving the saw blade the proper tension under all loads.

The table supporting the work is fastened to a casting directly above the lower wheel. It is slotted for the saw blade from the center to one edge. The guide prevents the blade from twisting sideways in the slot and gives it support when cutting. Design

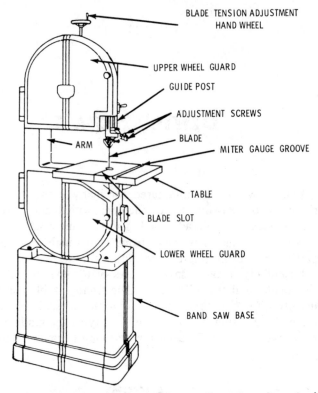

BLADE TENSION ADJUSTMENT
HAND WHEEL

UPPER WHEEL GUARD

GUIDE POST

ADJUSTMENT SCREWS

BLADE

MITER GAUGE GROOVE

ARM

TABLE

BLADE SLOT

LOWER WHEEL GUARD

BAND SAW BASE

Fig. 1. A typical band saw suitable for the small- and medium-sized woodworking shop. Tension and tilt are regulated by a convenient handwheel and a knob. The band saw gets its name from the blades used, which are continuous bands of steel.

varies for different types of saws. Some band-saw tables are equipped with a ripping fence, and some are also provided with a groove for a miter gauge.

The size of the band saw depends on the diameter of the wheels, which may vary in size from 10 to approximately 40 inches. So, a saw with 10-inch diameter wheels is called a 10-inch saw. Of course, the larger the wheels, the larger, in proportion, the other parts of the saw, and consequently, larger-size stock can be sawed. Other important dimensions of the band saw are the table size and the height between the table and the upper blade guide.

172

STRAIGHT-CUTTING OPERATION

Although a band saw is essential for curved cutting, it may also be used for making straight cuts for both crosscutting and ripping, where a table saw is not available. For all straight cuts, it is advisable to use the widest possible blade because it is easier to follow a straight line with a wide blade. The use of the miter gauge for crosscutting wide stock, as shown in Fig. 2, follows the same general procedure as that used for similar work on the table saw. In the absence of a miter gauge, a wide board with square ends and sides may be used, as shown in Fig. 3.

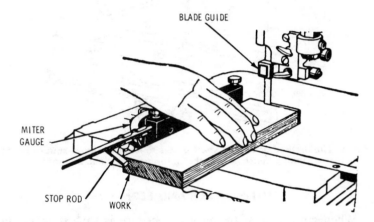

Fig. 2. Cutting to length with a miter gauge and a stop rod. The stop rod should be carried on the outer end of the miter gauge.

The use of an auxiliary wood fence fastened to the gauge will facilitate the handling of large boards and will result in more accurate work. Unlike the auxiliary ripping fence for the table saw, the wood fence for the band saw should be kept low so that it will work under the guides.

Ripping and resawing may be performed on a band saw by the use of the ripping fence furnished with most saws. When the stock is worked flat on the table, the operation is ripping, and when the board is worked on edge, the operation is usually known as resawing.

Another type of guide frequently used in these operations is known as the pivot block. The pivot block consists of a specially formed wood block that is clamped to the table to hold it in the desired position. The guide is set opposite the blade and at the proper distance from it to cut the required thickness, as shown in Fig. 4.

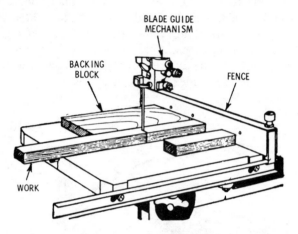

Fig. 3. *The method of cutting short pieces to length using a square board or a ripping fence, when the miter gauge is not available.*

CUTTING ARCS AND SEGMENTS

When cutting arcs, the usual procedure is to first make an outline by means of a compass or divider after determining the correct radius or diameter. If several pieces all having the same curvature are to be sawed, a jig may preferably be made, in which case the arcs can be accurately cut without having to make an outline.

MULTIPLE-SAWING OPERATION

To do the best work on a band saw, it is necessary to mount it on a substantial foundation to eliminate vibration. The blades must be kept in prime condition and must be properly adjusted on the wheels. When a considerable amount of wood is to be processed, an extension to the saw table is a real convenience, if not an actual necessity.

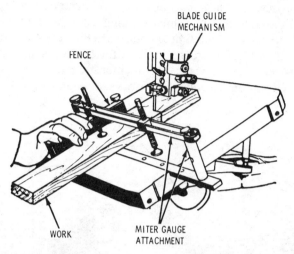

BLADE GUIDE
MECHANISM

FENCE

WORK

MITER GAUGE
ATTACHMENT

Fig. 4. Use of the miter gauge clamp attachment. An attachment of this type is useful in many crosscutting operations and particularly when cutting at an angle with the table tilted.

The numerous furniture parts frequently sawed in multiple include ornate chair and table stretchers, chair bannisters, radio-cabinet grilles, and small brackets. The grilles and similar items, however, are usually scrolled out on a jigsaw. Dependable machines are usually provided with accurate tension devices that assist the operator in securing volume production as well as turning out high-class work.

Some jigsaws are constructed with the table and saw guides set at such an angle with reference to the machine column that extremely long material may be sawed easily.

When cutting very thick material, best results may be obtained by sawing one piece at a time, particularly where there are pitch spots and checks and knots to be dodged. On the other hand, anywhere from 8 to 18 pieces of veneer or thin plywood can often be scrolled out simultaneously, depending on the thickness of the stock. Some favor the idea of tacking pieces together lightly before sawing, but a more satisfactory system is to cut two or more ³/₄-inch slits in their edges after stacking them up evenly on the saw table. A hardwood wedge driven into each of these slits will serve to hold the stock together while it is being processed. These two methods are illustrated in Fig. 5. It is not unusual to find workmen scrolling eight or more pieces of ¹/₂-inch plywood at one time without fastening the plies together in any manner. This procedure calls for considerable dexterity, and it is really not advisable to attempt it on work where great accuracy is essential unless the workman is an expert.

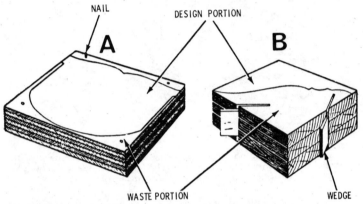

Fig. 5. The methods of assembly commonly used in multiple-sawing operations; A, nails are driven into the waste portions of the design to hold the parts together while being sawed; B, the stock is wedged together while being sawed.

POINTERS ON BAND-SAW OPERATION

In order to obtain the maximum quantity as well as the best possible quality from the band saw, it is necessary that the operator understand its operation and be able to adjust it properly. Prior to the actual sawing, the operator must be carefully versed in the various safety features with which the band saw is equipped. He should be familiar with the removal of the wheel guards, and before operating the band saw, should make certain that they are securely fastened. Some band saws are equipped with a braking device whereby the drive wheel may be stopped quickly for blade changes. Some types are provided with an automatic brake that instantly stops the wheels if the blade breaks.

It is a good idea to use the widest blade possible, giving consideration to the minimum radius to be cut on a particular class of work. A rule of thumb used by many is that the width of the blade should be one-eighth the minimum radius to be cut. Therefore, if the piece on hand has a 4-inch radius, the operator would select a $^1/_2$-inch blade. This rule should not be construed to mean that the minimum radius that can be cut is eight times the width of the blade, but rather that such a ratio indicates the practical limit for high-speed band-saw work.

Where the band saw is operated continuously, the blade tension may have to be increased gradually during the day because the heat of the blade will cause it to expand and stretch. As the blade expands, tension will decrease, and cutting will become more difficult. At the end of the day's work, the blade tension should be relieved, since the blade will contract as it cools and may fracture if the tension is too great. But this should not be a problem in occasional use.

The operator should also be able to select the correct blade for the class of work at hand. As previously mentioned, the widest blade possible should be used, taking into consideration the radius of the curves to be cut. The reason for this is that on straight or gently curving portions of work, it is much easier to follow the contour with a wide blade, since narrow blades often have a tendency to wander.

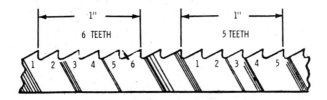

Fig. 6. The method of designating the number of teeth per inch.

Band-saw blades are commonly classified as 4-, 5-, 6-, or 7-tooth blades. This designation refers to the number of teeth per inch of blade length, as shown in Fig. 6. Where smooth cuts are desired, the 6- or 7-tooth variety should be used. Where speed is of more importance than the smoothness of a cut, a 4-tooth blade should be employed, because its larger teeth will cut more rapidly.

SUMMARY

Band saws are used for cutting curved outlines and lines not parallel to a straightedge. The type most adaptable to the general wood shop use is called a band scroll saw. They generally use a blade $1/2$ to 1 inch in width and 10 to 40 inches in diameter, depending on the diameter of the upper and lower drive wheel.

Although a band saw is excellent for curved cutting, it may also be used for making straight cuts for both crosscutting and ripping when a table saw is not available. When using a band saw for straight cutting, it is easier to follow a straight line with a wide blade.

REVIEW QUESTIONS

1. What is the big advantage in using a band saw?
2. How many teeth per inch on the common band-saw blade?
3. How should tension on the saw blade be checked?
4. How is straight cutting accomplished?
5. How is miter cutting accomplished?

CHAPTER 12

Jigsaws

The jigsaw differs in anatomy from the band saw, although the type of work for which it is designed is quite similar. The jigsaw is more adaptable than the band saw for cutting small, sharp curves simply because much smaller and finer blades may be used. Inside cutting is also better accomplished on the jigsaw, since the blade is easily removed and inserted through the entrance hole bored in the stock.

CONSTRUCTION

The jigsaw illustrated in Fig. 1 consists essentially of a base or frame, a driving mechanism, a table, a tension mechanism, guides, and a saw blade. The jigsaw that is part of a combination tool is shown in Fig. 2. The driving mechanism in a jigsaw has a motor-driven wheel that is connected by a steel rod to a bar, called the "cross-head," which moves up and down between two vertical slides. This arrangement converts the rotating motion of the motor into a reciprocating (up-and-down) movement of the blade and provides an efficient cutting action.

The table built around the blade is usually designed for tilting at angles up to 45°. The size of the jigsaw is generally expressed in terms of the throat opening, that is, the distance from the blade to the edge of the supporting arm. The distinguishing feature of saws of this type, as previously noted, is that the blade moves with a reciprocating motion instead of moving continuously in one direction, as in the case of table and band saws. Accordingly, only one-half the distance traveled by the saw blade is effective in cutting.

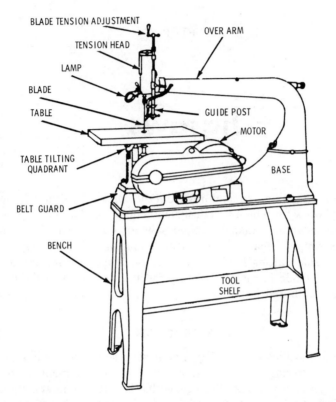

Fig. 1. The component parts of a typical jigsaw. A jigsaw of this type uses a 6-inch blade, but it can accommodate smaller and larger blades. The table can be tilted 45° either way and is equipped with a graduated quadrant showing the exact number of degrees of tilt. The upper head adjusts on dovetail ways by means of a hand crank and a knurled locknut. Blade tension is shown on a scale and may be regulated for minimum vibration while the machine is running. The drive mechanism is of the reciprocating type with link and counterbalanced crank. The air pump is powered by the main drive shaft and keeps the cutting line clear at all saw-blade speeds. The guides are adjustable for front and side sawing.

With the jigsaw and its numerous attachments, there are comparatively few cutting operations that cannot readily be accomplished. The primary uses of the jigsaw are for cutting out intricate curves, corners, etc., as in wall shelves, brackets, and novelties of wood, metal, and plastics.

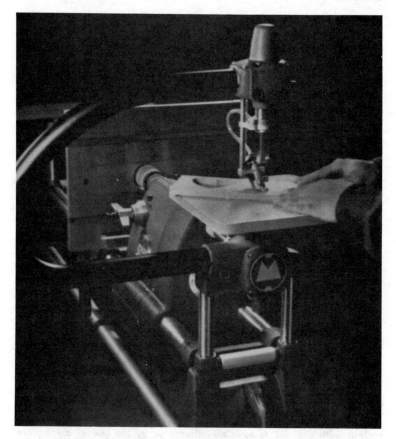

Fig. 2. This jigsaw is part of a combination tool. Wide throat allows manipulation of large stock. Courtesy of Shopsmith.

JIGSAW OPERATION

As mentioned, the jigsaw is primarily used for making various types of intricate wood cuttings that cannot readily be made on the band saw. The chucks are generally made to accommodate various sizes of blades, which are inserted with the teeth pointed in a downward direction. In operation, the front edge of the guide block should be in line with the gullets of the teeth and should be fastened in that position. The guide post is then

181

brought down until the hold-down foot rests lightly on the work to be sawed. For most work, the operation of the jigsaw does not differ in any important respect from that of the band saw.

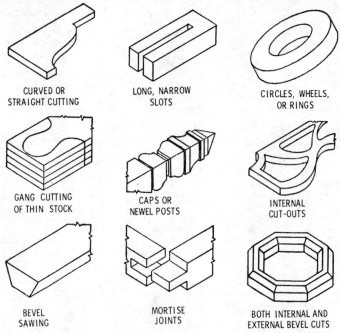

CURVED OR
STRAIGHT CUTTING

LONG, NARROW
SLOTS

CIRCLES, WHEELS,
OR RINGS

GANG CUTTING
OF THIN STOCK

CAPS OR
NEWEL POSTS

INTERNAL
CUT-OUTS

BEVEL
SAWING

MORTISE
JOINTS

BOTH INTERNAL AND
EXTERNAL BEVEL CUTS

Fig. 3. Various items produced by means of jigsaw cutting. One of the most important steps in cutting any shape from wood is that of marking pattern shapes on the wood to be cut. This is usually done by drawing the pattern with the aid of suitable squares or by the use of an outline projector. The pattern so produced can sometimes be mounted directly on the wood as a cutting guide, or else the pattern may be produced directly on the work by means of carbon paper.

The speed of the jigsaw is generally determined by the material to be cut, as well as the type of blade used, in addition to the skill of the operator. Various speeds of from 650 to 1700 cutting strokes per minute may be selected by the use of the proper step on the cone pulley. Jigsaw blades vary a great deal in length, thickness, width, and fineness of the teeth. All blades, however, may be grouped under two general classifications:

1. Blades gripped in both the upper and lower chucks.
2. Blades held in the lower chuck only.

The latter types of blades are known as saber blades (Fig. 4), whereas the former are called jeweler's blades. The jeweler's blades are useful for all fine work where short curves predominate, while saber blades are faster cutting tools for heavier materials and medium curves. When it is desirable to make inside cuts, a starting hole is normally drilled at a suitable location.

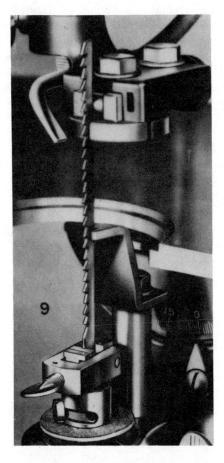

Fig. 4. Saber saw blades may be used without being chucked in at the top. This can be convenient when making certain cuts. Courtesy of Rockwell.

SUMMARY

The jigsaw and band saw generally do the same type of work, although the jigsaw is more adaptable to sharp curves because smaller and finer blades are used. The jigsaw can cut inside holes since the blade is easily removed and inserted through a hole bored in the wood.

The speed of a jigsaw is generally varied by selecting the proper pulley groove and is governed by the material used and the type of work to be done. The blades vary a great deal in length, thickness, width, and number of teeth per inch.

Blades are generally known as saber blades (which connect at only one end), and jeweler's blades (which connect at both ends). Since the blade action is an up-and-down motion, sharper corners can be made and more accurate work can be accomplished.

REVIEW QUESTIONS

1. What is the motion action of the jigsaw blade?
2. What are some of the advantages in the jigsaw over the band saw?
3. Name the two types of blades used in the jigsaw.
4. What is the throat opening on a jigsaw?
5. How is the speed change on a jigsaw accomplished?

CHAPTER 13

Wood Lathes

A wood lathe is a stationary power tool used for shaping wood. The wood revolves in the lathe while a sharp-edged cutting tool held in the hand and supported by a slide rest is pressed against it. Since the wood is revolving while being cut, the operation is termed *woodturning*.

The principal parts of a wood lathe, as shown in Fig. 1, are:

1. The bed.
2. The headstock.
3. The tailstock.
4. The tool rest.

The bed usually consists of a heavy casting that resembles two parallel V-ways and is supported by cast-iron legs on a table to bring the work up to the desired height. The two V-ways carry a rigid headstock at one end and a tailstock at the other, the latter arranged to slide on the V-ways and to be secured at any point by tightening the tailstock clamp. The headstock is bolted to the bed and contains the driving mechanism of the lathe. This consists of a hollow spindle supported between two bearings.

The spindle is revolved either by a step-cone pulley or by an individual motor, in which case the spindle is directly connected to the motor. As shown in Fig. 2, a spur center is fitted into the spindle and engages one end of the wood to be turned, the other end being secured by the tail center. The spur center turned by the belt drive on one of the steps of the cone pulley and the spurs on the center cause the piece of wood inserted between the centers to turn also.

185

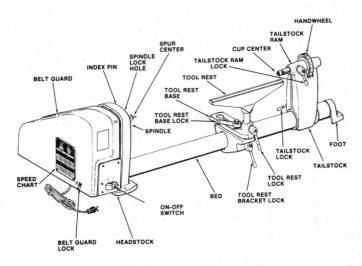

Fig. 1. Essential parts of the wood lathe.

Both the tool post and the tailstock can be clamped to the bed at any point desired. By resting a sharp-edged cutting tool against the T-shaped tool rest, the wood is shaved off and the surface reduced to a circular form.

LATHE SPEEDS

The lathe speed may be regulated in several ways, depending on the method of drive. When the lathe is driven from a set of step pulleys, the speed at the cutting edge will range from 1,000 to 2,500 feet per minute, depending on the type of turning to be done. When the headstock is directly motor driven, the speed is usually regulated by a rheostat or by a special switching arrangement that provides for up to four speeds, usually from 500 to 3,600 rpm. No definite rule for lathe speeds can be laid down, however, because of the large variations in diameter that often occur in the piece to be turned. Too slow a speed not only is a great waste of time but it will also leave a rough finish on the wood. Too fast a speed may damage the cutting tools. Always remember, the largest diameter of the material will determine the lathe spindle speed.

Fig. 2. *You should mount the lathe on a sturdy table, such as the one shown. Courtesy of Sears, Roebuck & Co.*

STARTING AND STOPPING THE LATHE

Prior to starting the lathe, the adjustments and clamps should be tested to assure their workability, and the work should be revolved by pulling the belt by hand to make sure that the work clears the tool post. It is better to start turning at a safe speed and increase it, if necessary, after the work is rough-turned and is running true.

The lathe should never be run at high speed if any part of the work is off center or out of balance. If the work to be turned is out of balance, it should be counterbalanced by suitable weights, although this may not always be possible. To stop the machine, the belt is shifted, or the motor is disconnected and braking is accomplished by placing the hand on the pulley. Large faceplate work, however, should not be stopped too suddenly in this way, as there is danger of unscrewing the plate from the spindle.

A smooth piece of work can be safely stopped by braking on the work itself, using a handful of shavings or smooth turnings to prevent burning. However, the lathe should never be stopped by placing the hand on the back or edge of the faceplate, since there are likely to be projecting objects on it that may cause injury to the operator.

LATHE ATTACHMENTS

Lathe attachments (Fig. 3) consist of several tools or accessories necessary to properly perform the work. They are *lathe centers, drivers, screw chucks, center chucks, faceplates*. Accessories include various *turning* and *measurement* tools.

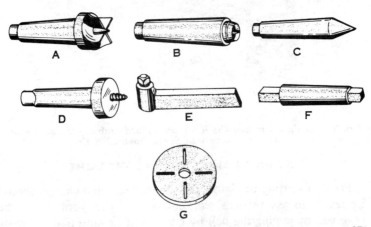

Fig. 3. *Lathe attachments: (A) Spur drive center; (B) Cup center; (C) Cone center; (D) Screw center; (E) Tool holder; (F) Adapter; (G) Faceplate.*

Lathe Centers

The function of the lathe centers is to hold the work and revolve it between the spindles. They are of three principal types—the *spur* or *live center*, the *headstock* or *tailstock center*, and the *cup center*.

The spur or drive center is used in the live spindle for driving small and medium-sized pieces that are to be turned between the centers. The spur center is tapered to fit the hole in the spindle, and the driving end has a point and either two or four spurs to engage the wood. The spur center is inserted in the piece to be turned by setting the point in the center and driving the spurs in by striking the end of the center with a mallet. The center is removed from the lathe by pushing a rod through the hole in the spindle.

The tailstock center is used to support the right-hand end of the work and is generally self-discharging. It may be removed from the spindle by drawing the spindle back with the hand-wheel as far as it will go. This action will automatically push the center out of the spindle.

The cup center is also a tailstock center and has a thin circular steel edge around a central point. It is more accurate than the cone center and does not split the wood so easily. Since the dead or tailstock center does not revolve, the end of the stock that turns on them should be well oiled to prevent burning by friction.

Lathe Drivers

Drivers are devices, other than the spur center, used for revolving the work. There are several forms available, with some made to be used with a small slotted faceplate and dog (as in machine-shop turning), the center plate having a projection to which the dog is fastened. Another form of driver is one in which the center has a square shank over which the dog fits.

Screw centers are small faceplates with a single screw in the center and are used for turning small pieces. Some screw centers hold the central screw firmly and have an attachment for regulating the projection of the screw through the face.

Faceplates are holding devices used for work that cannot readily be driven by any of the foregoing methods. They contain screw holes countersunk on the back for the screws used in fastening the wooden face or chuck plates. The smaller sizes are frequently provided with a recess in the center for rechucking purposes. They are made in various sizes, depending on the size of the lathe and the stock they must support. Objects such as circular disks, bowls, and trays are always turned on faceplates.

Woodturning Tools

Woodturning tools (Fig. 4) are used for cutting and scraping purposes, the most common of which are various types of gouges, chisels, and parting tools. Gouges are beveled on the outside or convex side, and the length of the bevel is about twice the thickness of the steel. Skew chisels are beveled on both sides, and their cutting edges form a 60° angle with one side of the chisel. Parting or cut-off tools are thicker in the center of the blade than at the edges and, thus, will not bind or overheat when a cut is made. This tool is used for making narrow cuts to a given depth or diameter.

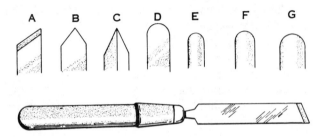

Fig. 4. Woodturning tools: (A) Skew chisel; (B) Spear-point chisel; (C) Parting tool; (D) Round-nose chisel; (E) Gouge; (F) Gouge; (G) Gouge.

Measurement Tools

Other necessary tools are those used for measurements (Fig. 5), usually termed sizing and layout tools. The tools for sizing and layout work on the lathe include both inside and outside calipers and dividers. Measuring rods are also used for sizing faceplate work, and are used for sizing both the inside and outside of a ring-formed object.

MEASUREMENTS

The ability to take accurate measurements plays an important part in woodturning work and can be acquired only by practice and experience. All measurements should be made with an accurately graduated scale.

An experienced operator can take measurements with a steel

scale and calipers to a surprising degree of accuracy. This is accomplished by developing a sensitive caliper feel and by carefully setting the calipers so that they split the line graduated on the scale.

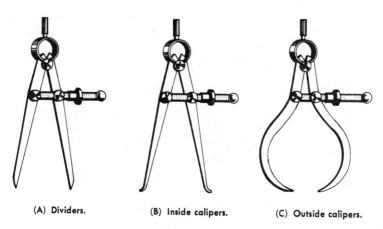

(A) Dividers.   (B) Inside calipers.   (C) Outside calipers.

Fig. 5. Measurement tools.

Outside Calipers

A good method for setting an outside caliper to a steel scale is shown in Fig. 6. The scale is held in the left hand and the caliper in the right hand. One leg of the caliper is held against the end of the scale and is supported by the finger of the left hand while the adjustment is made with the thumb and first finger of the right hand.

The proper application of the outside caliper when measuring the diameter of a cylinder or a shaft is shown in Fig. 7. The caliper is held exactly at right angles to the center line of the work, and is pushed gently back and forth across the diameter of the cylinder to be measured. When the caliper is adjusted properly, it should slip easily over the shaft of its own weight. Never force a caliper or it may spring and the measurement may not be accurate. Never grip the caliper too tightly; the sense of touch will be very much impaired.

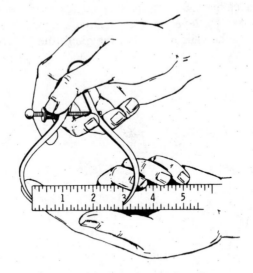

Fig. 6. Method of setting an outside caliper to a steel square.

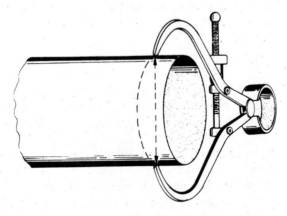

Fig. 7. Method of measuring with an outside caliper.

Inside Calipers

To set an inside caliper for a dimension, place the end of the scale against a flat surface and the end of the caliper at the edge and end of the scale. Hold the scale square with the flat surface.

Adjust the other end of the caliper to the required dimension, as shown in Fig. 8.

To measure an inside diameter, place the caliper in the hole, in the position shown in Fig. 9 by the dotted line, and raise the hand slowly. Adjust the caliper until it will slip into the hole with a very slight drag. Be sure to hold the caliper square across the diameter of the hole.

In transferring a measurement from an outside caliper to an inside caliper, the point of one leg of the inside caliper rests on a similar point of the outside caliper, as shown in Fig. 10. Using this contact point as a pivot, move the inside caliper along the dotted line shown in the illustration, and adjust with the thumb screw until you feel the measurement is just right. The hermaphrodite caliper shown in Fig. 11 is set from the end of the scale exactly the same as the outside caliper.

The accuracy of all contact measurements is dependent upon the sense of touch or feel. The caliper should be delicately and lightly held in the finger tips—not gripped tightly. If the caliper is gripped tightly, the sense of touch is lost to a great extent.

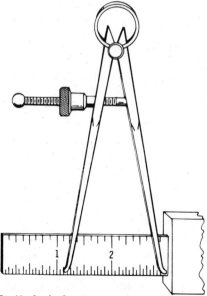

Fig. 8. Method of setting an inside caliper.

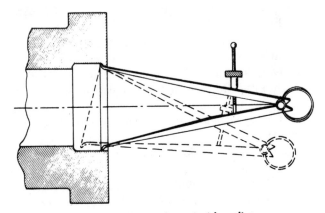

Fig. 9. Measuring with an inside caliper.

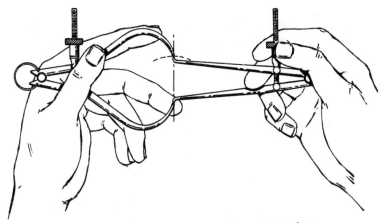

*Fig. 10. Transferring a measurement from an inside to an
outside caliper.*

CENTERING AND MOUNTING STOCK

Wood stock to be turned must be properly marked; that is, the
true centers must be obtained prior to turning. In square stock,
the center is usually determined by the diagonal method, which
consists of holding the center head of a combination square
firmly against the work and drawing two lines at right angles to
each other and close to the blade across each end of the work.

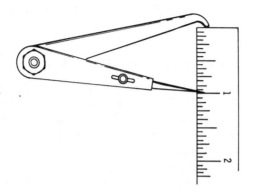

Fig. 11. Setting a hermaphrodite caliper.

After the work center has been marked, the work can be mounted in the lathe as shown in Fig. 12. The stock is first pressed against the spur or live center so that the spurs enter the grooves previously marked. Next move the tailstock up to about 1 inch from the end of the stock and lock it in this position. Then advance the tailstock center by turning the feed handle until the center makes contact with the work. Continue to advance the center while slowly rotating the stock by hand. After it becomes difficult to turn the stock, slack off on the feed about one-quarter turn and lock the quill spindle. The stock is now ready for turning.

The tool rest is next mounted in position so that it is level with the centers and about ⅛ inch away from the stock. Clamp the

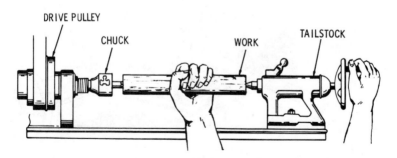

Fig. 12. Method of mounting work in a lathe.

tool rest in position and revolve the stock by hand to make certain it has sufficient clearance.

TYPICAL WOODTURNING OPERATIONS

The most common woodturning operations include such simple steps as roughing off, paring or finishing, squaring of ends, and making concave or ring cuts. In a roughing-off cut, place a large gouge on the rest so that the level is above the wood and the cutting edge tangent to the "circle of cut." In adjusting the rest for this, the handle of the gouge should be well down. Roll the gouge over slightly to the right so that it will shear instead of scrape the wood. Lift the handle slowly forcing the cutting edge into the wood. Remove the corners of the wood first, then the intervening portions. The tool should be held at a slight angle to the axis of the wood being turned, with the cutting end in advance of the handle, as shown in Fig. 13.

In making a paring or finishing cut, lay a skew chisel on the tool rest with the cutting edge above the cylinder and at an angle of about 60° to the surface. Slowly draw the chisel back and, at the same time, raise the handle until the chisel cuts about $1/4$ to $3/8$ inch from the heel. Begin the first cut about 1 to 2 inches from either end, pushing toward the other end. Then begin at the first starting point and cut toward the other end, thus taking off

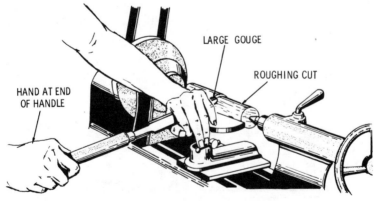

LARGE GOUGE

ROUGHING CUT

HAND AT END
OF HANDLE

Fig. 13. The correct way to hold a gouge in making a rough cut on the lathe.

the rings left by the gouge, and cutting down to where the scraped sections are just visible. Take a last cut to remove all traces of the rings and to bring the wood down to a uniform diameter from end to end. To test for smoothness, place the palm of the hand, with the fingers extended, lightly on the back side of the wood away from the tool rest.

After the work has been reduced to a cylinder, the ends may be squared to mark the end of the turning. This is commonly accomplished by placing the $1/4$- or $1/2$-inch skew chisel on the tool rest and bringing the cutting edge next to the stock perpendicular to the axis, as in Fig. 14. The heel of the chisel is then slightly tipped from the cylinder to give clearance. Raise the handle and push the chisel toe into the stock about $1/8$ inch outside the line indicating the end of the cylinder. Swing the handle still further from the cylinder and cut a half V to give clearance and prevent burning. Continue this process until the cylinder is cut through to about a $1/16$-inch diameter.

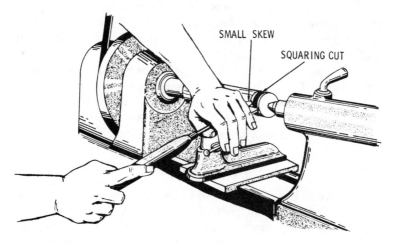

SMALL SKEW

SQUARING CUT

Fig. 14. A skew chisel is held in this manner to square the ends of the work.

When making concave cuts, place the gouge on the tool rest with the cutting edge well above the wood. Roll the tool to the side until the bevel at the cutting point is perpendicular to the axis of the cylinder. Slowly raise the handle to force the gouge

197

into the wood. When the gouge bites into the wood, force it forward and upward by slightly lowering the handle while rolling it back toward its first position. Reverse the position of the gouge and make a similar cut from the other side to form the other half of the semicircle.

Ring cuts are made by placing a $1/4$- or $1/2$-inch small skew chisel on the tool rest with the cutting edge above the cylinder and the bevel tangent to it. Draw the chisel back and raise the handle, bringing the heel of the chisel in contact with the cylinder at the marked line. The chisel is then moved to the right (if cutting the right side of the bead) while being continually tipped to keep the lower bevel tangent to the revolving cylinder and to the head at the point of contact. Continue the cut until the bottom of the convex surface is reached.

POLISHING

The polishing of turned work in the lathe is a great deal easier than applying polish to a flat surface. Here, the polishing operation is done with a cloth while the work is rotating in the lathe and after it has been sanded.

In sanding, first use a fairly coarse grade of paper, followed by a fine grade. Before applying the polishing cloth, the wood may be varnished lightly while the lathe is not running, taking care to wipe off all surplus varnish. The varnish will assist in giving the surface a fine polish when the cloth is applied.

SUMMARY

The principal parts of a wood lathe are the bed, headstock, tailstock, and the tool post. The headstock and the tailstock support the wood which is being turned. The tool post supports the chisel or gouge which cuts or shapes the wood being turned.

There are many woodturning tools, both for cutting and for measuring. Cutting tools include skew chisels, spear-point chisels, parting tools, round-nose chisels, and gouges. The skew chisel is beveled on both sides, and forms a cutting edge of 60°.

REVIEW QUESTIONS

1. Name the four main parts of the cutting portion of a wood lathe.
2. What is the difference between inside calipers and outside calipers?
3. What is the difference between dividers and calipers?

CHAPTER 14

Planers, Jointers, and Shapers

Three tools that tend to be specialized in their uses but that can prove to be invaluable in the shop are the planer, the jointer, and the shaper. The chief function of each is to shape wood, but each does more.

THICKNESS PLANER

The planer (Fig. 1) is more properly called the *thickness planer,* and this name describes one of its main functions. It has the ability to take rough stock and make it smooth. The thickness planer has a cutter with three planer knives that surface stock up to a certain width. A common size is $12\frac{1}{4}$ inches wide and up to 6 inches thick. Basically, you feed the rough board in at one end and it comes out smooth at the other end.

Another job the planer can do is edge-mold: make a tongue-and-groove edge on boards. This can be valuable because it allows you to make flooring, sheathing—whatever you wish—where tongue-and-groove stock is normally used.

The thickness planer can also face-mold. You set the machine for cutting the stock to width, then put a particular edge on it, depending on the cutterheads used. In other words, you can make your own molding (Figs. 2, 3, 4).

One other function is as a board-ripping machine. The Belsaw 910, for example, can rip stock up to $2\frac{1}{4}$ inches thick and, of course, surface it to desired thickness in a single pass (Fig. 5).

Fig. 1. A thickness planer. Courtesy of Belsaw.

The thickness planer is really only a tool for the carpenter, builder, or very active handyman, or perhaps for someone who owns a woodworking shop. It is not an inexpensive machine, and before you were to buy one, you would want to be sure that there was enough work to justify the cost.

JOINTERS

The jointer is similar to the planer except that it has only one cutter head located below the table, and the feed is usually by hand. Its primary use is to cut a true face and edge on stock that is warped, twisted, or has other irregularities. The table is in two sections, the in-feed section being raised or lowered to control the thickness of the cut. The out-feed part of the table is raised or lowered by a unit to control the thickness of the finished piece. By tilting the fence, bevel edges can be cut. This machine can also be used for tapering, end planing, and rabbeting.

Fig. 2. Face molding is one operation performed by the planer. Courtesy of Belsaw.

Construction

The essential parts of a jointer (Fig. 6) consist of a *base* or frame supporting the assembly, *cutter head, tables or bed, guide fence,* and *table-adjusting hand wheels.*

The cutter head houses two or more high-speed steel knives and revolves between the front or in-feed table and the rear or out-feed table. The tables may be raised or lowered by means of hand wheels to regulate the depth of cut.

A guide fence extends along both tables to hold the work as it is advanced toward the cutting knives. The fence may be tilted 45° either way and may also be moved crosswise along the jointer table. The cutter head is generally provided with a guard cover as a safety measure.

Adjustments

One of the most important adjustments on the jointer is the relation of the rear table to the cutter head. To do satisfactory

Fig. 3. *The planer rips stock up to 2¼ inches thick and surfaces it at the same time. Courtesy of Belsaw.*

work, this table must be exactly level with the knives at their highest point of rotation. To make this adjustment, follow manufacturers' instructions. Fig. 7 shows the correct and incorrect positions of the rear table.

The in-feed table, on the other hand, must be somewhat lower than the rotating knives, the exact height of which depends upon the depth of the cut. The difference in height between the two tables is equal to the depth of the cut. Improperly adjusted tables will result in the work being cut on a taper.

When knives become dull or nicked, it is necessary to either replace them or sharpen them. Jointing knives may be sharpened and brought to a true cutting circle by jointing their edges while the cutter head is revolving. In performing this operation, a fine-cutting oilstone is placed on the out-feed table, and the table lowered until the knives just touch the stone at their highest point of rotation. It is easier for the neophyte to replace blades.

Fig. 4. Planing is being done here. Courtesy of Belsaw.

Operation

Although a great number of woodworking operations may be performed on the jointer, the most common are edge planing, planing of ends, and surfacing (Figs. 8, 9, 10). Among these, edge planing or jointing an edge is the simplest and most common operation. Assuming the machine to be properly adjusted, and the guide fence square with the table, all that is necessary is to feed the work over the rotating cutter heads. The left hand presses the work down on the rear table so that the cut surface will make a good contact with the table. The right hand exerts no downward pressure on the front table, but simply advances the work over the knives. Both hands, however, exert pressure on the work to force it against the guide fence to obtain the proper edge.

Edges on thin work, such as veneer, may also be planed on the jointer provided the work is held firmly between two suitable

Fig. 5. Edge molding is another function of the planer. Courtesy of Belsaw.

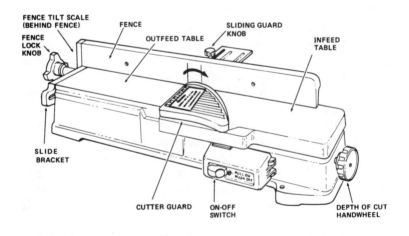

Fig. 6. Parts of a joiner.

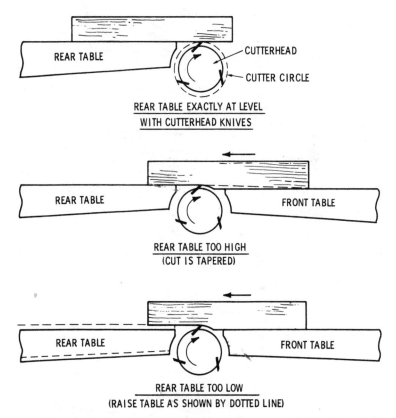

Fig. 7. *Showing the effect of rear-table adjustment on the jointer. The rear table must be adjusted until it is exactly level with the cutter knives at their highest point of rotation. The front table is lowered by the amount of the desired cut.*

boards or planks. In most edge-planing operations of this type, special clamps are used to hold the work in place.

Planing across the ends of boards may be performed in a manner similar to planing with the grain. The necessary precaution consists in taking only light cuts each time because of the tendency of the grain at the end of the board to split if thick cuts are attempted. To avoid splitting the end wood, some operators make only a short cut at one edge, then reverse the wood and complete the planing from the opposite edge.

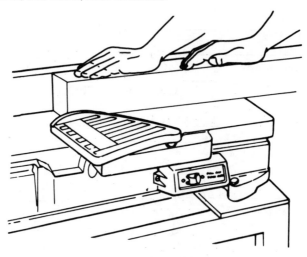

Fig. 8. Hand-over-hand motion is best when jointing stock over 3 inches thick.

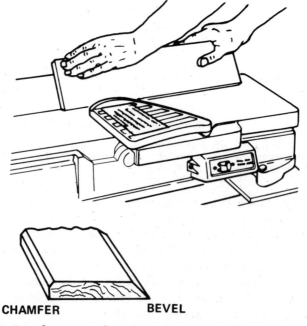

CHAMFER   BEVEL

Fig. 9. Keep fingers together when edge jointing. Note edged boards.

Surfacing the faces of a board is one of the more difficult jointer operations. When planing the faces, the grain pattern in the edges should be noted. To plane the board with the grain, the two sides of the board must be planed in opposite directions.

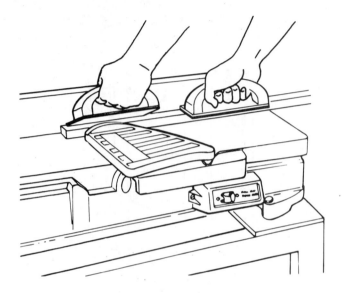

Fig. 10. When stock is small, guards should be used.

SHAPERS

A shaper (Fig. 11) is used mainly to place an edge on stock having an irregular outline (Fig. 12), and for rabbeting, grooving, and fluting. Some of the cuts that can be made are shown in Fig. 13.

A shaper consists essentially of one or more vertical spindles with cutting heads, table, fence, and base. Generally, a knife with its cutting edge ground to the desired shape of cut is used, but solid cutters milled to the desired shape are also available.

Stock may be cut roughly to shape with a band saw or jigsaw before being finished on the shaper. When a number of pieces of the same pattern are to be shaped, special templates or forms are often used to regulate the depth of cut by bearing against the shaper collar.

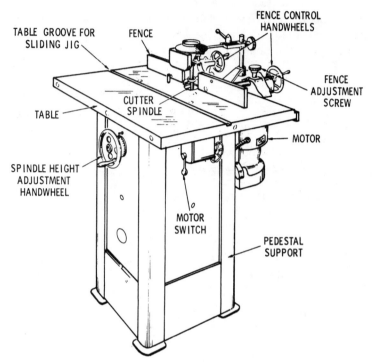

Fig. 11. A typical shaper.

Anatomy

Shapers are usually constructed with one or more vertical spindles, which carry the cutter heads. Two spindles revolving in opposite directions are perhaps the most general and useful form, since one cutter can cut with the grain of wood running in one direction and the other cutter can operate on wood with the grain running in the other direction without stopping to reverse the machine.

The spindle (Fig. 14) projects above the surface of an accurately planed table. Cutters are attached to this spindle, and the assembly rotates at speeds of 5,000 to 10,000 rpm or higher. On account of this high speed, pulleys of about three-to-one ratio are generally necessary when the machine is driven by a standard 3,600 rpm motor.

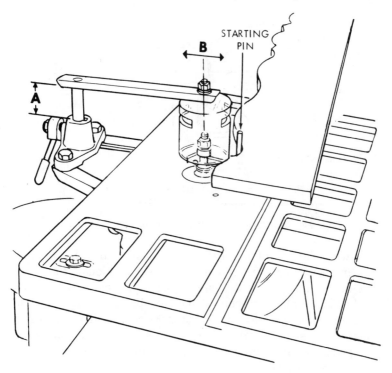

Fig. 12. One operation of the shaper.

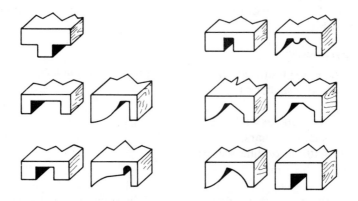

Fig. 13. Some of the many cuts that can be made on a shaper.

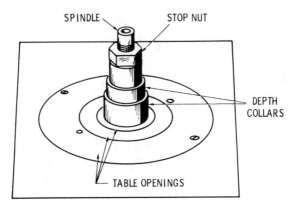

Fig. 14. The shaper spindle projects through the table.

A wide variety of knives, saws, collars, etc., are used in shaper operations. Shaper knives are of two kinds—the open-face or flat knives, and the three-lip cutters. The flat knives are used mainly on large machines, and have beveled edges which fit into corresponding slots milled in two collars. The knives of exactly the same width are always used, and they must be clamped securely to prevent them from loosening while the machine is in operation.

The three-lip shaper cutters have three cutting edges, and slip over the spindle shaft. This type of cutter is much safer to work with. Fig.15 illustrates some of the various types of cutters available.

Operation

There are four main methods used to hold or guide the stock against the shaper knives:

1. With guides or fences.
2. Against collars.
3. With an outline pattern.
4. With forms.

Each one of these methods is widely employed and each is suitable for a certain kind of work. Fig. 16 illustrates the use of

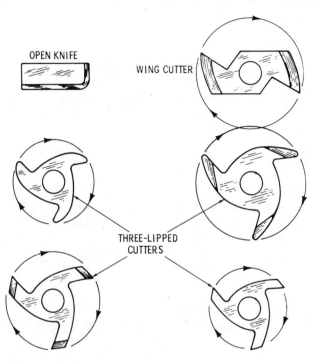

OPEN KNIFE

WING CUTTER

THREE-LIPPED
CUTTERS

Fig. 15. Various types of cutters are available for use on a shaper.

these four methods. In Fig. 16A, the work is held against a fence as it is advanced into the cutter. The position of the fence thus determines the depth of cut. This method is used only for straight cuts. (Adjustment of a shaper fence is shown in Fig. 17.) In Fig. 16B, the depth of cut is regulated by a collar—a deeper cut requires a collar with a smaller diameter. The edges of an irregularly shaped piece of material can be cut using this method. The use of an outline pattern is shown in Fig. 16C. With this method, the pattern rides against the collar to determine the depth of cut. Fig. 16D shows a form being used to hold the work in position so that it can be advanced to the shaper cutter.

Where a job calls for working the stock directly against an ordinary shaper collar (such as in Fig. 15), the friction created between the collar and the work has a tendency to burn and mar the material. This burning can be avoided, however, by using a

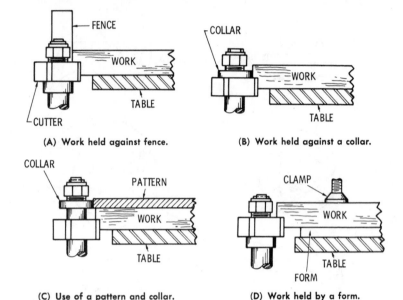

(A) Work held against fence.   (B) Work held against a collar.

(C) Use of a pattern and collar.   (D) Work held by a form.

Fig. 16. Four principal methods used to hold the work against the shaper knives.

ball-bearing guide collar in place of the regular type. The outer shell of the ball-bearing collar revolves independently of the inner shell, and thus rolls along with the feed, practically eliminating all wear and friction on any forms or guide patterns being used or on the material being shaped.

Heavy cutting is best accomplished with open-faced knives set in open collars, with the assembly being well balanced to avoid vibration to render the setup as safe as possible. Whenever it is necessary to work directly against the shaper collar, it is well to rest the stock against a steel guide-pin, while easing it slowly to the knives at the beginning of each cut. If the character of the work is such that it is impossible to employ a hold-down device, two or more light cuts should be made where considerable material is to be removed. It is advisable to relieve the cut as much as possible by chamfering off the corners of the stock with a band saw on which the table can be tilted, or on a tilting-blade bench saw. The equipment that is really best adapted to extra-heavy cutting is the type of shaper with overhead bearings, although some operators prefer a machine having an auxiliary drop table.

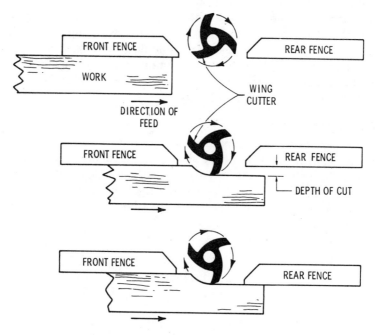

Fig. 17. Adjustment of shaper fences.

In the type of operations employed in the average millwork shops, shaping with guides is a very popular method. The most common types of guides are various fences to suit the particular operation desired. Capable operators keep an ample supply of fences on hand, each usually being adapted to one particular class of work. These generally include one for chamfering, another for grooving, and still others for panel raising, rabbeting, and other setups called for most frequently. When using a saw on the shaper spindle for grooving, it is customary to tack a strip of plywood panel stock on the face of the fence, which is then positioned so that the blade cuts through the plywood the proper distance to make the required depth of groove.

When milling short and light work, the strips of hardwood that serve as guard and hold-down can sometimes be used as a fence. This is because it is readily set at any required distance from the cutters by means of the adjusting screws.

When machining curved and irregular-shaped parts, some operators use small curved fences equipped with adjusting rods that fit into the regular guard and hold-down device. They usually find this method better than working the stock against the shaper collar, as the friction produced by the latter method frequently burns and glazes the stock.

Power and Speed

The size of the motor necessary to operate a shaper depends upon the type of work to be done. The medium-sized shaper using 1/2-inch hole cutters works satisfactorily with a 1/2-horsepower motor. In cases where large knives mounted between slotted collars are used, a 3/4- to 1-horsepower motor will be necessary.

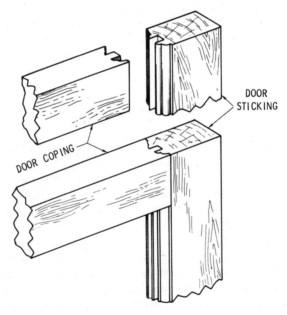

DOOR STICKING

DOOR COPING

Fig. 18. A shaper is used to form the parts of a door.

The motor must be a 3,450-rpm type in order to give the shaper spindle the required speed. With a pulley ratio of 3 to 1, the actual spindle speed will be in the order of 10,000 rpm. The motor should preferably be of the reversible type, since an opposite direction of rotation may often be required.

A few of the many shapes that are cut by using a shaper are shown in Figs. 18, 19, and 20.

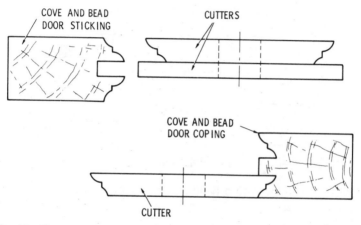

Fig. 19. *The same cutter is used to form both mating sections of a door.*

SUMMARY

A planer is a stationary tool used to plane wood by means of removing the rough surface. The wood to be planed is passed under the cutting heads, leaving a smooth or finished surface. Many machines are available with two cutting heads so that both sides of a piece of lumber may be planed in one operation. A planer is generally power fed which means the lumber is automatically fed into the cutting heads.

The jointer is very similar to the planer, except it has only one head generally located below the table. The lumber is usually fed by hand. The primary use of the jointer is to cut a true surface on lumber that is warped or twisted.

A shaper is used to finish the edge on stock lumber, and for rabbeting, grooving, and fluting. Many times, stock may be cut

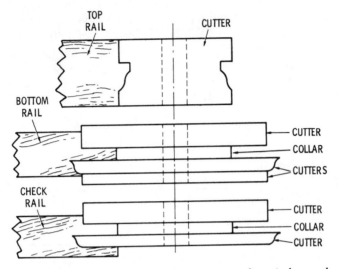

Fig. 20. Shaper cutters used to form the parts of a window sash.

roughly to shape with a band saw or jigsaw before it is finished on the shaper.

REVIEW QUESTIONS

1. Explain the difference between a planer and jointer.
2. What are the principal operations of a shaper?
3. How many cutting heads are used on a planer?

CHAPTER 15

Radial Arm Saw

Some craftsmen consider the radial arm saw to be the most important stationary power tool, even ahead of the bench saw or table saw, which is favored by many.

In fact, the radial arm saw (Fig. 1) does all the things a table saw does. With the table saw, however, you move the work into the revolving saw blade; with the radial arm saw, the saw, which is suspended on an arm, is moved into the work.

For example, if you are doing a crosscutting operation, the work is set on the table, then the saw is turned on and moved across the work, severing it neatly.

The radial arm saw is also capable of many other cuts. Most commonly there is the rip cut—cutting stock lengthwise. Here, the work is moved into the blade, which is stationary. It is also common practice for the workpiece to be supported on an extension table of some sort so that it is manageable.

The saw, complete with motor, can be tilted so that it can make miter cuts, crosscut bevel cuts, and others. Like the table saw, the radial arm saw may be equipped with a dado head for making grooves in stock. In this case, instead of feeding the work into the blade, the dado head is drawn across the stock.

OTHER ATTACHMENTS

The radial arm saw may be equipped with a variety of attachments that can be used for drilling holes, sanding, drum sanding, and buffing.

Figs. 2 to 5 show a variety of operations that can be performed with the saw.

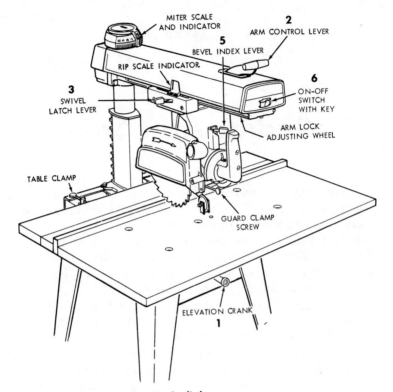

Fig. 1. Radial arm saw.

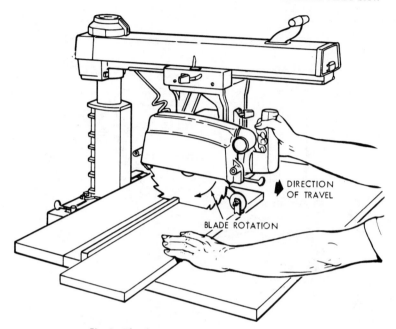

DIRECTION
OF TRAVEL

BLADE ROTATION

Fig 2. The basic operation is crosscutting.

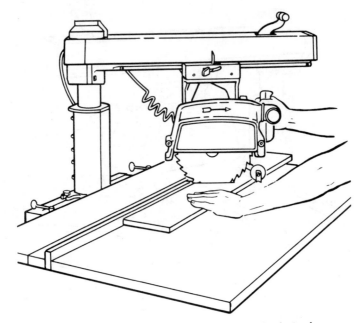

Fig. 3. Miter crosscut. Saw is set to angle desired.

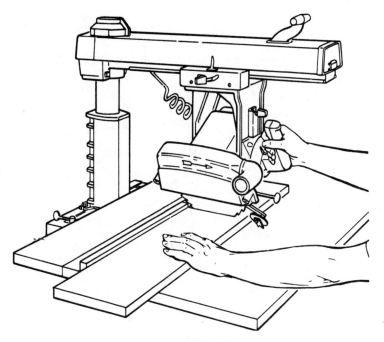

Fig. 4. Bevel crosscut.

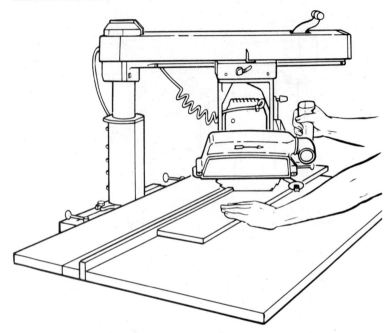

Fig. 5. Compound crosscut.

CHAPTER 16

Sanders and Combination Tools

Sanders play an important role in all kinds of carpentry and woodworking. You can sand by hand or use a portable sander (detailed in Chapter 18). Or you can use a stationary sander, of which there are three main types: the belt sander, the disk sander, and a combination of the two. These three sanders are discussed here, as is another machine, which is commonly known as a combination tool and has a number of functions, one of which is sanding.

DRUM SANDERS

Drum sanders are generally large production machines used to sand large items such as doors, plywood panels, and other types of flat work. The drum sander is also frequently used to surface the faces of panel frames (after assembly of the frames on jigs) after gluing in order to smooth out any slight differences in adjoining frame members, which might cause gaps in the glue bond.

The drum sander is built on the principle of a planer but, in place of the cutter heads, has one or more rotating sanding drums.

BELT AND DISK SANDERS

The combination belt and disk sander (Fig. 1) is used chiefly for cabinet work and other small stock. The disk table may be

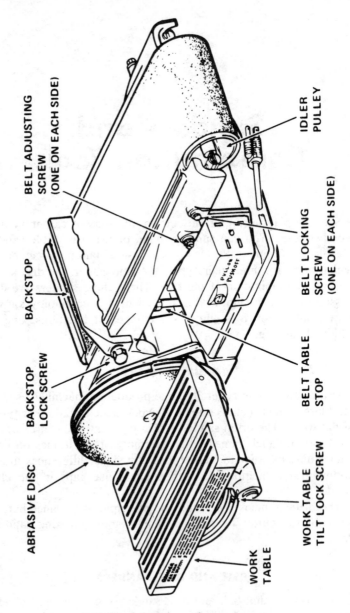

Fig. 1. Belt-disk sander anatomy.

moved up and down and tilted to any angle from 0° to 45°. It is also fitted with gauges for grinding compound angles, for making duplicate pieces, and for finishing circular pieces of various radii. The disk sander may be used for much circular work which is turned in the lathe, and also for many operations for which the planer and jointer are used. A separate belt sander is shown in Fig. 2 and a disk sander in Fig. 3. A typical use of a disk sander—sanding end grain—is shown in Fig. 4.

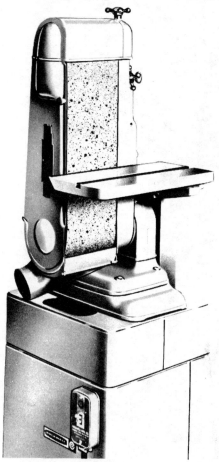

Courtesy Rockwell Manufacturing Company, Power Tool Division

Fig. 2. A typical belt sander.

The use of the miter gauge is shown in Fig. 5. By using this gauge in combination with the tilting table, it is comparatively simple to obtain any combination of angles desired on the work.

A miter table is also provided for the sanding belt. By using this table and miter gauge, angles can be sanded on the belt, as shown in Fig. 5.

Fig. 3. Disk sander.

Fig. 4. A disk sander being used to sand the end grain of a piece of wood.

COMBINATION TOOLS

There are a number of brand names for these tools; the most common, and perhaps so common that it has become synonymous with the tool, is the Shopsmith.

The combination tool has a sanding function—disk sanding—but it has four other functions: lathe, table saw, borer, and drill press. The Shopsmith machine uses one motor that is capable of speeds from 700 to 5,200 rpm with a dial setting for speeds desired.

The combination tool does a good sanding job, and works well on its other jobs, but some people dislike the nagging task of having to set up the machine separately for each of the various tools to be put into action. Indeed, for some people this negates the tool's worth.

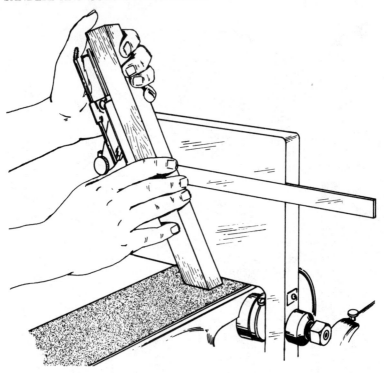

Fig. 5. *Use of the vertical table and miter gauge to sand the end of a piece of wood. The table assures an accurate surface that is 90° with relation to the sanding belt. The miter gauge determines the accuracy of the bevel.*

The combination tool's disk sander is used like a regular disk sander; its other tool functions are performed in the usual manner, too. Additionally, you can obtain a tremendous variety of attachments for the tool that can make it perform virtually any job. You should not, however, expect its motor to be as hearty as motors on individual power tools.

SUMMARY

The function of a sanding machine is to smooth the wood surface by a scratching action of various types of abrasives. These abrasives come in a wide variety of sizes, shapes, and coarseness.

Fig. 6. Combination tool. Courtesy of Shopsmith.

There are various types of sanding machines, such as drum, belt, and disk. Drum sanders are generally large production machines used to sand large items such as doors, plywood panels, and other large flat work. Certain drum sanders are designed to sand or finish both top and bottom surfaces of a board simultaneously.

A combination belt and disk sander is used mainly for cabinet work and other small jobs. The disk sander is used for circular work and various angles. Generally, the sanding table can be moved up and down or tilted to any angle up to 45°. Gauges are also used to grind or sand compound angles or for making duplicate pieces.

REVIEW QUESTIONS

1. Name the various types of sanding machines.

231

2. Name the sanding machine used for cabinet work or for various angles.
3. What is a combination tool?

Chapter 17

Drill Press

For precision drilling of holes, a drill press is really the only tool you should consider. Its anatomy is indicated in Fig. 1. Essentially it consists of a drill that rides up and down—controlled by a feed lever—on a solid column. The workpiece is placed on a table (that can be raised or lowered as desired), and the hole is drilled. The size hole you drill depends on the bit you use with the tool. The size of the drill press itself is determined by the diameter of the circle of the workpiece. From the center of this piece to the column determines size. Hence, if the distance from the center of the table to the column is 10 inches, a 20-inch disk can be fitted on the table, and the tool is characterized as 20 inches.

The speed of the drill press is controlled by the belt, which is looped over a couple of pulleys, as well as the rpm of the motor itself.

The drill press is also capable of routing and shaping, but these are secondary rather than main functions. Its main function is to drill holes of various sizes with precision.

The speed range of a drill press depends upon the size and number of pulleys, as well as the speed of the driving motor or shaft. In a typical machine equipped with a four-step cone pulley, the speed may be varied from 600 to 5,000 rpm. The speed of a machine used exclusively for metalworking ranges between 400 and 2,000 rpm.

BORING TOOLS

All cutting tools used for making holes in wood are called *bits*, whereas similar tools used for metals are called *drills*. A distinc-

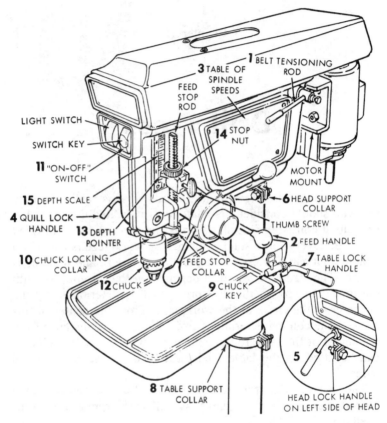

Fig. 1. Drill press.

tion is sometimes made in the cutting operation, the term *boring* applying to holes made in wood, while *drilling* means a cutting operation in metal. The most common type of machine boring bits are the *auger* and *twist-drill*. Other types are the *center* and *expansive bit*, each of which has its particular application in the woodworking shop.

Auger bits (Fig. 4A) are equipped with a central screw that draws them into the wood, two ribs that score the circle, and two lips or cutters that cut the shavings. These are used for boring holes from $1/2$ to 2 inches. The sizes are listed in 16ths; thus a 2-inch auger is listed as a number 32.

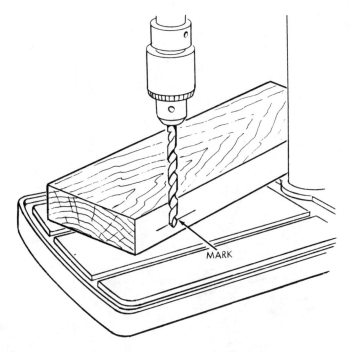

Fig. 2. Blind drilling of holes is easy with a drill press. Just set the bit to go down a certain amount.

A twist drill differs from an auger in the absence of a screw and a less acute angle of the lip; hence there is no tendency to split the wood. In other words, the tool does not pull itself in by a taper screw but enters by external pressure. Twist drills are used for boring small holes where the ordinary auger would probably split the wood. They come with either round or square shanks and in sizes from $1^1/_{16}$ to $^5/_8$ inch or larger, varying by 32nds.

The center (Fig. 4B) and expansive bits (Fig. 4D) are used for boring large holes. The center bit is used primarily for boring holes through material which might split with bits of other types, whereas the expansive bit is adjustable and is used for boring large holes of various diameters, usually up to 3 inches. Another type of boring device is the Forstner bit (Fig. 4C).

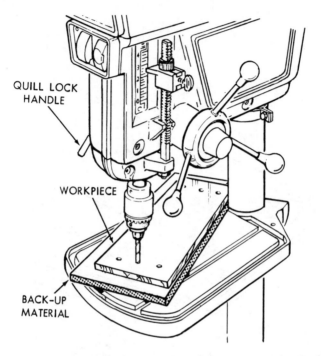

Fig. 3. *When drilling through a material, a back-up piece of material is a good idea. It avoids splintering on the far side of material.*

SUMMARY

Essentially a drill press consists of a vertical spindle having a chuck at one end and a telescoping splined sleeve with a drive pulley on the other. A table is placed under or in front of the chuck to hold the work.

The size of the boring machine depends on the size of work to be bored and the speed of the drill. The cutting tools used for making holes in wood are called bits.

REVIEW QUESTIONS

1. What is a drill?
2. What is a bit?

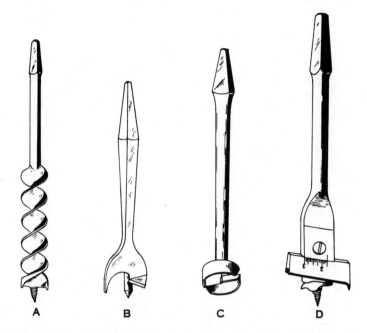

A B C D

Fig. 4. *Various types of bits for boring holes in wood; (A) Auger bit; (B) Center bit; (C) Forstner bit; (D) Expansion bit.*

3. Explain the purpose of a drill chuck.
4. What is the difference between an auger bit and an expansion bit?

CHAPTER 18

Portable Power Tools

It has been estimated that a carpenter using a circular saw can cut up ten times more wood, in the same amount of time, as a carpenter using a hand saw. This is a rather startling fact, and points up one of the great advantages to using portable power tools: They make jobs that might be tiresome much easier.

There are a couple of other advantages. For one thing, the possibility or probability of precision work is greater, simply because one uses power.

Job for job, portable power tools cannot compare with stationary power tools; the latter are simply better. But unless special arrangements can be made, stationary tools often cannot go where portable tools are used.

Following is a roundup, in no particular order of importance, of common portable power tools. Note, too, that while some manufacturers provide tools with grounded plugs, others make them with plastic housing, which is a defense against electric shock and should be seriously considered when shopping for portable power tools.

PORTABLE SAWS

For the cutting of large panels, the circular saw (Fig. 1) is usually the way to go. These saws come in a variety of sizes with the size designated by the diameter of the blade the saw can accept. A blade about 7 inches in diameter is about right for most craftsmen. This means it can cut stock a little less than half the diameter of the blade—slightly less than $3^{1}/_{2}$ inches.

Fig. 1. Circular saw with carbide-tipped blade.

Portable saws, like other power tools, come with variable speeds, meaning that pressure on the trigger regulates the speed at which the blade rotates. You can get blades to cut virtually anything, including stone. Slowing or speeding the rpm of the blade is a factor here.

Using the saw is not difficult, but as with all power tools, you have to be careful.

With the switch in the off position, rest the front edge of the saw base flat on the work. Start the saw by pulling back on the trigger switch and begin the cut, being careful not to jam the saw blade into the work suddenly. Forcing may place an unnecessary strain on the operating parts, which may possibly require their premature replacement. For most cutting operations, guiding the saw through the work is all that is necessary. If the motor should stall due to a dull blade or unnecessary pressure, do not release the switch at once, but pull the saw back, allowing the blade to run free before shutting off the motor. This precaution reduces burning of the contact points in the switch and greatly lengthens its life.

240

Power Source

Before connecting the cord plug to an electrical outlet, be sure that the line voltage is the same as that stamped on the nameplate of the tool. When an extension cord is necessary, it should be of sufficiently heavy wire to assure full voltage at the tool with the machine under load.

ELECTRIC DRILLS

The process of drilling holes in metal and boring holes in wood with an electric drill (Fig. 2) is similar to drilling or boring by hand, except that the power for turning is furnished by an electric motor instead of by the operator. Drills of this type usually

Fig. 2. Electric drill. It can be fitted with many attachments.

have capacities for drilling holes from $^1/_{16}$ inch up to 3 inches in diameter.

Operation

To use an electric drill, first mark the location of the hole. Then, with the motor running, insert the point of the drill on the mark and start drilling. Care must be used to hold the electric drill at right angles to the work so that the hole will be straight. With the tool held in this manner, exert a light pressure and continue drilling; use variable speed feature as needed.

If the hole is to go completely through the work, relieve the pressure on the drill when the point of the drill bit begins to break through and until the hole is completed. Finally, withdraw the drill from the hole by pulling it straight back, and then shut off the motor.

Twist drills do not pull themselves into the work; they must be fed by pressure, and this pressure must be exerted by the operator of an electric drill in exactly the same way as if drilling entirely by hand. The only effort saved the operator by the electric drill is that of turning.

BENCH GRINDERS

Bench grinders are commonly used in woodworking shops for sharpening chisels, screwdrivers, etc., and for smoothing metal surfaces. Fig. 3 shows a common type of bench grinder. This type of grinder consists mainly of an electric motor having a double-ended horizontal spindle, the ends of which are threaded and fitted with flanges to take the grinding wheels. Other models employ a conventional belt drive.

The size of the grinder is commonly taken from the diameter of the abrasive wheel used in connection with it. Thus, a grinder with a 6-inch diameter wheel is called a 6-inch grinder. Grinder units are further classified as bench or pedestal, the latter indicating a floor model.

A bench grinder is usually fitted with both a medium-grain and fine-grain abrasive wheel. The medium wheel is satisfactory for rough grinding where a considerable quantity of metal has to be removed, or where a smooth finish is not important. For

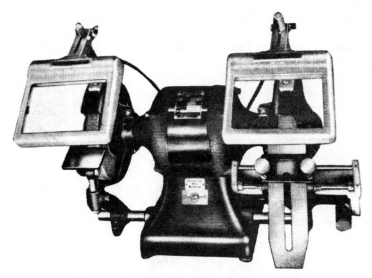

Fig. 3. A bench grinder used to sharpen tools.

sharpening tools or grinding to close limits of size, the fine wheel should be used, as it removes metal slower, gives the work a smoother finish, and does not generate enough heat to anneal the cutting edges. When grinding tools, keep a pan of water handy, and dip the tool in it often to assure against overheating.

When a deep cut is to be taken on work, or when a considerable quantity of metal must be removed, it is often practical to grind with the medium wheel first and finish up with the fine wheel. The wheels are removable, and most bench grinders are so made that wire brushes, polishing wheels, or buffing wheels can be substituted for the grinding wheels.

Operation

In grinding, the work should be held firmly at the correct angle on the rests provided and fed into the wheel with enough pressure to remove the desired amount of metal without generating too much heat. The rests are removable, if necessary, for grinding odd-shaped or large work. As a rule, it is not advisable to grind work requiring heavy pressure on the side of the wheel, as the pressure may crack the wheel. As abrasive wheels become

243

worn, their surface speed decreases and this reduces their cutting efficiency. When a wheel becomes worn in this manner, it should be discarded and a new one installed on the grinder.

Safety Precautions

Before using a bench grinder, make sure that the wheels are firmly held on the spindles by the flange nuts, and that the work rests are tight. Wear goggles, even if eye shields are attached to the grinder, and bear in mind that it is unsafe ever to use a grinder without wheel guards. Wearing glasses does not take the place of wearing goggles. A pair of expensive glasses is easily ruined, as the flying sparks stick to the glass and sometimes can not be polished off. Also, remember that it is easy to run a thumb or finger into the wheel.

ELECTRIC PLANES

In finish carpentry work, the use of a plane is often necessary. For example, in fitting doors, it is usually necessary to plane one or more edges to obtain the proper clearance between the door and its jamb. A plane is also a necessity when cabinets are built on the job, and for the installation of various other items, such as book shelves.

Electric planes are now available to perform much of the work formerly done with hand tools. An electric plane, such as the one shown in Fig. 4, provides an accurate and rapid means of planing and, in most instances, will result in more precise work with less effort. The model shown is adjustable for depth of cut and has a side fence that can be set to plane any desired angle. When set at 90°, the planed edge will be at a true right angle to the side of the material. The plane in Fig. 4 has a 3-inch cutter, which is more than adequate for most work.

SABER SAWS

Another good addition to the carpenter's tool collection is the saber saw (Fig. 5). Most models are capable of cutting through 2-inch stock with ease (though it is better to use a circular saw for this) and can be used in places impossible to reach with an

Fig. 4. Electric plane.

electric hand saw. The real value of the saber saw lies in the intricate shapes it can cut in plastic, wood, and even metal by using the proper type of blade. The cut can be adjusted to any desired depth and angle.

A full-range of blades is available for this type of saw, from the standard combination blade, for rough cuts in wood, to metal-cutting blades. Even knife-edge blades for cutting leather, fabric, etc., may be purchased. Accessories are also available. These include fences for accurate straight-line cuts, circle-cutting attachments, and offset blade chucks to permit sawing flush with a wall or sawing up to an object.

SANDERS

A tool that eliminates much of the drudgery from finishing and at the same time produces a better finish is the portable electric sander. There are many types of these handy machines available—the orbital sander, reciprocating sander, and the belt sander. Of the three, the belt sander, such as the one in Fig. 6,

Fig. 5. A saber saw is good for curve cutting.

provides the most rapid removal of material. Orbital or finishing sanders (Figs. 7 and 8) are better suited for final finishing work, however. All grades of grit are available for the belts and sheets used with these machines. The sander shown has a belt that is 4^1/$_2$ inches wide.

THE ROUTER

Many carpenters will tell you that they might be able to get along without some other power tools, but not without the router. It is a versatile, valuable tool (Fig. 9).

Basically, a router consists of a canister-shaped housing with a bit projecting out of the base. The bit revolves at tremendous speeds. The operator grips handles on the sides of the canister and runs the router along the material. The bit cuts.

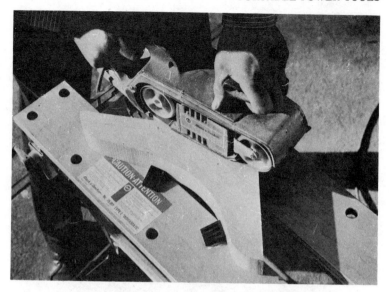

Fig. 6. Belt sander.

Routers can be fitted with a variety of bits including ones that make it invaluable in trimming plastic laminate, crosscutting or ripping stock, and making ploughs or grooves in boards and plywood.

As with other tools that use bits, router bits come in a variety of materials. Carbide-tipped ones are more expensive but last far longer than plain steel and are acknowledged as well worth the extra cost.

SUMMARY

Power-operated hand tools include electric hand saws, hand planes, routers and mortisers, air and electric hammers, portable drills, bench grinders, and hand sanders. Many of these tools have taken the disagreeable jobs out of carpentry work.

Power hand saws are very easy to operate and are made to cut material up to approximately 4 inches thick, depending on the size of the saw. It should be noted that, although very easy to operate, this type of power tool can be dangerous in operation

Fig. 7. Orbital sander.

due to suddenly jamming the saw blade into the wood. Generally, saws are equipped with combination blades for general-purpose work, but special blades for ripping, crosscutting, mitering, dadoing, metal cutting, etc., are available.

Drilling holes in metal or boring holes in wood with an electric drill is similar to drilling or boring by hand, except that power for turning is furnished by an electric motor instead of by the operator. Many drills can be fitted with attachments for driving

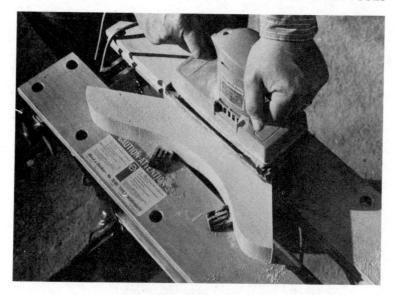

Fig. 8. Finishing sander.

Fig. 9. Router.

screws, rotating small grinders, drilling at right angles, etc. Many drills can be mounted on a drill stand, which provides an easy control for feeding the drill into the work.

REVIEW QUESTIONS

1. Name a few power-operated hand tools.
2. What are some advantages in using a saber saw?
3. Why are saw blades manufactured for the power hand saw?
4. Name the three types of portable hand sanders.
5. What are some advantages in using an electric plane?

CHAPTER 19

Termite Protection

At certain times of the year, termites develop wings, emerge from the ground in swarms like bees, and fly away to form new colonies. Winged termites and winged ants look somewhat alike, but they have definite differences, as seen in Fig. 1. Termites have a straight body and four milky-white wings, all of equal length and twice as long as the body. Swarming ants also have four wings, but they are transparent and of unequal length, the longest only half again as long as the body. Termites have short, straight, beaded antennae, while the antennae of ants are elbowed, with a bead-like end.

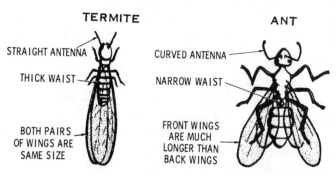

Fig. 1. Termites and ants differ in several respects.

Termites prefer to enter a building through cracks in the foundations or through the cavities in a hollow wall. When these avenues are not available, they will build mud tunnels up from the ground to the wooden parts of the building. These tunnels will be on the surface of the walls (usually on the dark interior side), or back of a pile of lumber, brick, or other materials stacked against the foundation. They are great engineers, however, and have often been known to build hollow tubes up from the ground for a foot or more to reach edible wood. Porch floors consisting of a concrete slab over a fill are fruitful sources of termite troubles, and exceedingly hard to eradicate. It may necessitate drilling through the floor and injecting heavy doses of toxic chemicals. It may be necessary to do the same where concrete drives or walks contact foundations.

In any case of termite infestation, it is probably best to employ a competent pest-control firm. Termites are tricky.

Each year termites do millions of dollars worth of damage, more than the combined loss from arson, tornadoes, and lightning, and more than twice the damage they caused only ten years ago. Measures to assure their control are becoming more and more necessary. Some of the methods used have not proved to be entirely satisfactory. Certain woods are susceptible to *Lyctus* (powder-post) beetles. If a powdery substance is noticed coming from small holes, these beetles have attacked the wood.

TERMITES AND THEIR IDENTIFICATION

There are several kinds of termites, but the ones that do the most damage are of the subterranean species. This type lives in the ground but travels into wood that is in contact with the soil, or into wood that is close enough to the soil to permit building mud tunnels through which they can reach the wood. The presence of these tunnels is sometimes the first sign of a termite infestation. Only a few species of timber are immune to termite damage. Heart cypress and redwood have some slight immunity, but even these woods are occasionally attacked. These termites do not seem to bother very resinous heart wood of long-leaf southern pine, but this kind of timber is not always available. Pressure-treated with a suitable preservative, all species of timbers are entirely immune to termite attack.

Termites are often found in stumps or posts and other wood in contact with the soil, but even though such infestations are very near a house, it does not imply that the house is, or will be, infested. Termites seldom leave a location of their own accord, and they work very slowly. There is no need to panic when they are discovered, for the damage, to a great extent, is already done. A delay of even several months is usually of little consequence.

CONSTRUCTION TO PREVENT TERMITE DAMAGE

Termites must maintain contact with the ground to obtain the moisture necessary for their existence. Hence, the first consideration should be to build in a manner that will prevent the entry of termites from the ground. The foundations of buildings should be constructed either of masonry or of approved pressure-treated or naturally termite-resistant lumber. Where a basement is provided, the foundation walls should be of masonry. If unit-block construction is employed, such as brick, tile, or cement blocks, all joints should be well filled with mortar and the wall topped with a 4-inch cap of concrete. This should be reinforced to prevent cracking when over open-type units. The ground within the basement should be sealed over with concrete; posts should not extend through the floor into the soil, but should rest on concrete footings that extend at least 2 inches above the floor.

If foundations are built over an earth fill or naturally loose earth, subsequent settlement may cause the joints between the concrete basement floor and foundation walls to open up. Such joints are a probable source of termite entry and should be guarded against by installing mastic or metal expansion joints between the walls and floor. Concrete for basement floors and walls should be a dense mixture and the walls reinforced with steel rods at the corners and intersections to tie them together. Improper construction of the basement floor and walls may cause cracks to develop through which termites may gain free access from the earth. Window sills and frames in the basement should not come in direct contact with the ground, nor should leaves or debris be allowed to collect and remain in contact with them.

Buildings that have no basements should have the sills set a minimum of 18 inches and preferably 24 inches above the excavated ground or natural grade at all points to afford the necessary clearance and good ventilation. This is shown in Fig. 2. On the exterior, the building clearance to woodwork may be reduced to 8 inches above the finished grade line, provided the foundation walls permit access to occasional inspection for shelter tubes by the homeowner. In the case of solid foundations, ventilation should be provided by allowing not less than 2 square feet of net open area for every 25 linear feet of wall. Openings should be screened with 20-mesh noncorroding screening. All lumber that comes in contact with the ground should be pressure-treated with a preservative.

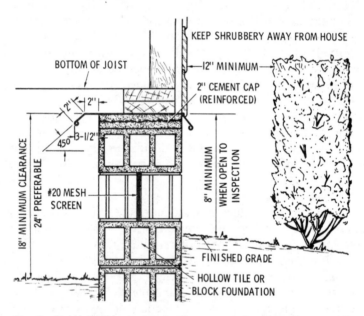

Fig. 2. Metal shields used in various types of construction to protect against an invasion of termites.

TERMITE SHIELDS

As pointed out, termites require constant access to soil moisture, and unless they stay in a moist atmosphere, they soon die. Because of this need for moisture, termites construct shelter tubes of earth or waste material to carry moisture and to act as passageways between the ground and their food supply when it is not in contact with the soil. Destroy or prevent this ground contact, and the termites cannot damage the building.

Termites may build these shelter tubes over the face of stone, concrete, brick, or timber foundations, and along water pipes or similar structures. Such contacts may be prevented by means of a metal shield barrier. This termite shield consists of aluminum firmly inserted and pointed into a masonry joint or under the sill. It projects horizontally at least 2 inches beyond the face of the wall and then is turned downward an additional 2 inches at an angle of 45°. All joints should be locked (and preferably soldered also), with the corners made tight and the outer edge rolled or crimped to give stiffness against bending, as well as to eliminate a sharp edge. The termite shield can also be bedded in asphaltum.

The termite shield should be used on each face of all foundation walls, except that it may be omitted from a face (either interior or exterior) exposed and open to easy and ready inspection. However, around houses and places where shrubbery may

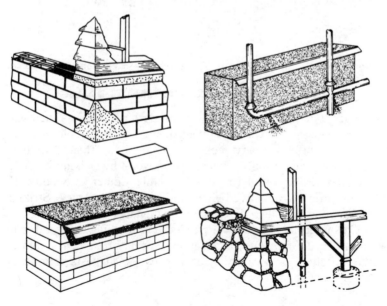

Fig. 3. A termite shield on top of a hollow foundation wall in a building with no basement.

partly conceal the wall and inspection is likely to be infrequent, a modified shield may be used. Here, the horizontal projection is omitted and the 2-inch projection bent downward at 45° is employed. Metal termite shields are required by many codes and by some city ordinances. Fig. 3 shows some typical termite shields. A method of inserting shields to prevent the passage of termites by the way of wooden porch steps is shown in Fig. 4.

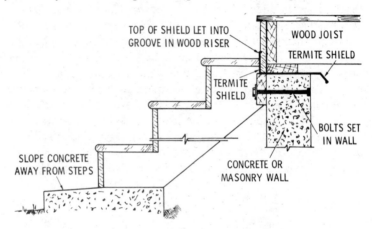

Fig. 4. Location of a termite shield between wooden steps and a porch.

DETECTING AND LOCATING TERMITE DAMAGE

Except at swarming time, termites are hidden unless their galleries or passageways are broken open. The earth-colored shelter tubes offer a ready means of recognizing their activities. Their work can usually be detected in wood by striking it with a hammer. Solid wood rings clear, while timber or woodwork eaten out by termites will give a dull thud when struck. Striking with an ice pick also determines weakened wood.

Clean-cut holes in books, papers, and clothing are good indications of the presence of termites. Springy basement floors or the softening or weakening of woodwork suggests termite or other damage.

STOPPING TERMITE DAMAGE

The most lasting and effective remedy for termite damage is to replace any wood in or near the basement of the building with concrete. Second in order of effectiveness and durability is to replace wood sections with treated wood or timbers and, in regions of excessive termite damage, to employ protective termite shields. By this means, contact between the colony and the building is permanently broken and relief from termite damage is assured. This means that joists embedded in concrete, wooden basement floors, and baseboards should be replaced with any type of plain or ornamental concrete. In basement rooms so constructed, movable furniture of wood, and also built-in furniture, particularly if resting on concrete footings, can be employed with safety.

To cap and face basement walls of frame buildings, it is rarely necessary to jack up the building. It is usually possible to remove the upper tier of brick or upper portion of the masonry unit in sections and replace with Portland-cement mortar and a suitable cap of slate or mortar. Where poor grades of mortar have been used in masonry walls below the ground, it may be necessary to coat the outside and, if necessary, the inside of the wall with concrete to keep termites from boring through.

USE OF SOIL POISONS

The use of chemicals is one of the most effective means of termite control. Its success lies in preparing a complete chemical barrier, which leaves no point of entrance for the termites. Two of the most effective and least expensive of the preparations used for this purpose are *chlordane* and *dieldrin*. Both are toxic and have been outlawed in some states. It is best to check local laws before using any chemical.

SUMMARY

There are several types of termites, but the ones that do the most damage are of the subterranean species. This type lives in the ground and travels to wood through tunnels. The presence of mud tunnels is sometimes the first sign of termite infestation. Heart cypress and redwood have a slight immunity, but even these woods are occasionally attacked.

Termites must maintain contact with the ground in order to

survive; moisture has to be accessible. The first consideration should be to build in a manner that will prevent the entry of termites from the ground. A foundation of any building should be constructed either of masonry or of approved pressure-treated or naturally termite-resistant lumber.

Where a basement is provided, the foundation walls should be of masonry. If construction of basement walls is of block, all joints should be filled with mortar and the wall topped with a 4-inch cap of concrete.

A termite shield may be installed under the foundation sill to prevent termites from entering the wood. This is a noncorroding metal shield that projects horizontally at least 2 inches beyond the foundation wall and then is turned down at a 45° angle an additional 2 inches. Corners must be tight with the outer edge crimped to give stiffness.

The use of soil poisons is another effective means of termite control. Two chemicals most commonly used are chlordane and dieldrin, which are poured into V-shaped trenches against the foundation walls. However, these are illegal in some states, and before using any chemical, the legality of its use should be checked out.

Review Questions

1. Name several ways to prevent termite damage.
2. What are two chemicals used in the ground to prevent termites from entering?
3. What should be done to the top row of blocks in a foundation to prevent termite damage?
4. Name two woods that have a slight immunity to termites?
5. What connection must a termite have with respect to ground?

Chapter 20

Painting

Painting can be a deceptive trade. It seems like the techniques required are simple to master and that, therefore, a typical painting job will be simple. But such is not really the case. While the techniques are not complicated, using the right ones, along with using the right materials, can make the difference between having a job look very good or not good at all (Fig. 1).

USING A BRUSH

The use of a brush assures good contact with surface pores, cracks, and crevices. Brushing is particularly recommended for applying prime coats and exterior paints.

In selecting a brush you should choose one that is wide enough to cover the area in a reasonable amount of time. If you are painting large areas such as exterior or interior walls or a floor, you will want a wide brush—probably 4 or 5 inches in width (Fig. 2). If you are painting windows or trim, you will want a narrower brush—probably 1 to 1½ inches in width.

The bristles should be reasonably long and thick so that they will hold a good load of paint; and they should be flexible so that you can stroke evenly and smoothly (Fig. 3). Generally speaking, a medium-priced brush is the best investment if you do only occasional jobs.

Paint should be brushed up and down, then across for even distribution. On a rough surface, however, it is wise to vary the direction of the strokes so that the paint will penetrate thoroughly. Make your finish strokes straight up and down.

Fig. 1. Paint can do a marvelous transformation job. Courtesy of Thomas Strahan Co.

The brush should be held at a slight angle, and pressure should be moderate and even. Excessive pressure or "stuffing" the brush into corners and cracks can damage the bristles.

Always start painting at the top of a surface and move downward. For interior painting, do ceilings and walls first, then the doors, windows, and trim areas. If floors are to be painted, they should be done last. And work toward the "wet edge" of the previously painted area—about 18 inches away—making sure not to try to cover too large a surface with each brush load.

Brush Care

A good brush is an expensive tool, and it pays to invest the necessary time and effort to take care of it properly. Clean paint

Fig. 2. A 4-inch brush is right for most craftsmen. Courtesy of Benjamin Moore.

brushes immediately after use with a thinner or special brush cleaner. Use turpentine or mineral spirits to remove oil-base paints, enamels, and varnish; alcohol to remove shellac; and naptha or lacquer thinner to remove lacquer. Remove latex paints promptly from brushes with soap (soap is the key) and water. If paint is allowed to dry on a brush, a paint remover or brush-cleaning solvent will be needed (Fig. 4).

USING A ROLLER

For large, flat surfaces, painting by roller is easier than painting by brush for the average do-it-yourselfer; many professionals still prefer a brush. Select a roller with a comfortable-to-hold handle and try several dry sweeps across the surface until you get the hang of it.

When you buy a roller set, it consists of the roller itself plus a sloping metal or plastic tray. Pour paint into the tray until approximately two-thirds of the corrugated bottom is covered.

Dip the roller into the paint in the shallow section of the tray,

Fig. 3. Brush should be loaded about halfway when painting. Courtesy of Benjamin Moore.

and roll it back and forth until it is well covered. If the roller drips when you lift it from the tray, it is overloaded. Squeeze out some of the paint by pressing the roller against the grid on the upper part of the tray above the paint line.

Apply paint by moving the roller back and forth over the surface being painted, first up and down in long, even strokes, then across. Reload the roller with paint as needed. Finish with vertical strokes (Fig. 5).

Roller Care

Rollers used with alkyd or oil-base paints should be cleaned with turpentine or mineral spirits. When latex paint has been used, soap and water will do a satisfactory cleaning job. If paint

Fig. 4. A clean brush will last for years. Soap is the key when cleaning a latex brush. Courtesy of Benjamin Moore.

has been allowed to dry on the roller, a paint remover or brush-cleaning solvent will be needed.

USING A SPRAYER

Paint sprayers are particularly useful for large areas. Spraying is much faster than brushing or rolling, and although some paint will likely be wasted through overspraying, the saving in time and effort may more than compensate for any additional paint cost. Once you have perfected your spraying technique, you can produce a coating with excellent uniformity in thickness and appearance.

Surface areas accessible only with difficulty to brush or roller can readily be covered by the sprayer. All coats can be applied satisfactorily by the spray technique, except for the prime coats. Spraying should be done only on a clean surface since the paint may not adhere well if a dust film is present.

Preparation of the paint is of critical importance when a

Fig. 5. Long nap roller is good for painting textured surfaces.

sprayer is to be used (Fig 6). Stir or strain the paint to remove any lumps, and thin carefully. If the paint is lumpy or too thick, it may clog the spray valve; if it is too thin, the paint may sag or run after it is applied. Follow the manufacturer's instructions on the paint label for the type and amount of thinner to use.

Before you begin, ask your paint dealer to show you exactly how the sprayer works, and to give you pointers on how to use it to best advantage. For best results:

1. Adjust the width of the spray fan to the size of the surface to be coated. A narrow fan is best for spraying small or narrow surfaces; a wider fan should be used to spray table tops or walls.
2. Before spraying, test the thickness of the paint, the size of

Fig. 6. Clean paint is important when spraying. Dip stick in and see how the paint flows. Courtesy of Benjamin Moore.

the fan, and the motion of the spray gun. Excessive thickness can cause rippling of the wet film or lead to blistering later.

3. Hold the nozzle about 8 inches from the surface to be painted.
4. Start the stroke or motion of the hand holding the sprayer while the spray is pointed slightly beyond the surface to be painted. This assures a smooth, even flow when you reach the surface to be coated.
5. Move the sprayer parallel to the surface, moving with an even stroke back and forth across the area. Spray corners and edges first.

265

6. Use a respirator to avoid inhalation of vapors.
7. Cover everything close to the work area with dropcloths, tarps, or newspapers. The "bounce-back" from a sprayer may extend several feet from the work surface. Outside, airborne spray can travel quite a distance.

Sprayer Maintenance

Clean sprayer promptly before the paint dries. After using oil-base or alkyd paints, clean the sprayer with the same solvent used to thin the paint. After using latex paint, clean with detergent and water. Fill the sprayer tank with the cleaning liquid and spray it clean.

If the fluid tip becomes clogged, it can be cleaned with a broom straw. Never use wire or a nail to clear clogged air holes in the sprayer tip.

HOW MUCH PAINT?

You can roughly figure the amount of paint you need for flat surfaces by simply multiplying the height (or length) times the width and dividing the result into the coverage estimate on the label. If, for example, you wish to paint a room that has 416 square feet of wall area, a gallon of paint advertised as covering 500 square feet will be adequate for one coat. Second coats generally require less paint.

However, these are only average estimates of coverage. Some surfaces are more absorbent than others.

PREPARATION TIPS

Before you brush, roll, or spray, there are certain preparations you should make to ensure a good job with a minimum of effort, errors, and spattering. The precautions may seem obvious, but they are often overlooked.

Protect other surfaces—Cover floors and furnishings with dropcloths. You can use tarps, old sheets, or the inexpensive plastic sheets designed for the purpose (Fig. 7).

Clean up as you paint—Wet paint is easy to remove; dry paint is hard to remove. Use turpentine or other thinner to remove oil

Fig. 7. Moving furniture to room center and covering it up as shown is a good idea for an interior job.

paint, water to remove latex. If paint is dropped on an asphalt tile floor, do not attempt to remove it with mineral spirits or turpentine because this may permanently damage the tile. If the paint will not come off with a damp cloth, let it dry and then scrape it off.

Rub protective cream or vaseline onto your hands and arms—A film of this cream will make it easier to remove paint from your skin when the job is done. Old gloves or throwaway plastic gloves and aprons are also useful.

Check the condition of the paint—When you buy new paint of good quality from a reputable store, it is usually in excellent condition. Nevertheless, after stirring the paint thoroughly, you

267

should examine it for lumps or color separation. Do not use the paint if there are any signs of these conditions.

On removal of the container lid, old paints release a foul odor (especially latex paints) or show signs of lumps or curdling. These paints are probably spoiled and should be discarded.

If there is a skin on the surface of the paint when you open the container, remove as much of the hardened film as possible with a scraper or knife and strain the paint through a cheesecloth or fine wire mesh such as window screening. If you fail to do this, bits of the skin will show up with exasperating frequency to spoil the appearance of your paint job.

New paints are usually ready for use when purchased and require no thinning unless they are to be applied with a sprayer. Get the advice of the dealer when you buy the paint, and check the label before you mix or stir. Some manufacturers do not recommend mixing as it may introduce air bubbles.

If mixing is required, it can be done at the paint store by placing the can in a mechanical agitator—or you can do it at home with a mixing stick.

If you open the can and find that the pigment has settled, use a clean paddle and gradually work the pigment up from the bottom of the can, using a circular stirring motion. Continue until the pigment is thoroughly and evenly distributed, with no signs of color separation.

If the settled layer should prove to be hard or rubbery, and resists stirring, the paint is probably too old and should be discarded.

Protect the paint between jobs—Between jobs, even if it is only overnight, cover the paint container tightly to prevent evaporation and thickening, and to protect it from dust. Oil-base and alkyd paints may develop a skin from exposure to the air.

When you finish painting, clean the rim of the paint can thoroughly and put the lid on tight. To ensure that the lid is airtight, cover the rim with a cloth or piece of plastic film (to prevent spattering) and then tap the lid firmly into place with a hammer.

Preparing the Surface

The finest paint, applied with the greatest skill, will not produce a satisfactory finish unless the surface has been prepared properly. The basic principles are simple. They vary somewhat with different surfaces and, to some extent, with different paints; but the goal is the same—to provide a surface with which the paint can make a strong, permanent bond. In general:

1. The surface must be clean, smooth, and free from loose particles such as dust or old paint. Use sandpaper, a wire brush, or a scraper (Fig. 8).

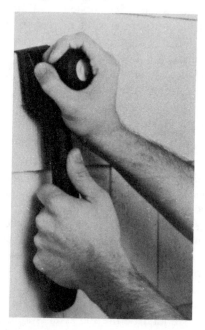

Fig. 8. Scrape off all loose paint before painting. Courtesy of Stanley.

2. Oil and grease should be removed by wiping with mineral spirits. If a detergent is used, it should be followed by a thorough rinse with clean water.
3. Chipped or blistered paint should be removed with sandpaper, a wire brush, steel wool, or a scraper.
4. Chalking or powdered paint should be removed with a stiff bristle brush or by scrubbing with water mixed with household washing soda or TSP (trisodium phosphate, sold in

hardware stores). If the old surface is only moderately chalked and the surface is relatively firm, an oil primer can be applied without the prior use of a stiff brush. The primer rebinds the loose particles and provides a solid base for the paint.

5. Loose, cracked, or shrunken putty or calk should be removed by scraping.
6. If new glazing compound, calking compounds, and sealants are used, they should be applied to a clean surface and allowed to harden before paint is applied. If the calk is a latex type, latex paint can be applied over it immediately without waiting for the calk to harden.
7. Damp surfaces must be allowed to dry before paint is applied, unless you are using a latex paint.

Preparing Wood

1. Scrape clean all areas where sap (resin) has surfaced on the wood, and sand smooth prior to application of "knot sealer." Small, dry knots should also be scraped and thoroughly cleaned, then given a thin coat of sealer before applying wood primer.
2. Fill cracks, joints, crevices, and nail holes with glazing compounds, putty, or plastic wood and sand lightly until the spots are flush with the wood. Always sand in the direction of the grain—never across it.
3. New wood surfaces to be stain-finished should first be sanded smooth. Open grain (porous) wood should be given a coat of paste filler before the stain is applied (paste fillers come in various matching wood colors). The surface should be resanded. Read manufacturers' instructions carefully before applying paste fillers.

Preparing Masonry

Surfaces such as plaster, gypsum, cement, and drywall should be dry and clean. If the surface is cracked, sand it smooth and then fill with spackling compound or some other recommended crack filler. After the repaired surface is dry, sand lightly until smooth, then wipe clean.

1. Allow new plaster to dry for 30 days before painting.
2. Roughen unpainted concrete and stucco with a wire brush to permit a good bond between the surface and the paint.
3. Wash new concrete surfaces with detergent and water to remove any film left over from oil or from the compound used for hardening the concrete during the "curing" process.
4. Remove "efflorescence," the crystalline deposit that appears on the mortar between the bricks in a brick wall, by using undiluted vinegar or a 5 percent muriatic acid solution. After scrubbing with acid, rinse the surface thoroughly.

Caution: When using muriatic acid, wear goggles and gloves for protection.

Painting Metal

1. Clean new metal surfaces such as galvanized steel, aluminum, or tin with a solvent such as mineral spirits to remove the oil and grease applied to the metal as a preservative by manufacturers.
2. Remove rusted or corroded spots by wire brushing or with coarse sandpaper. Chemical rust removers are also available from paint and hardware stores. Paint will not adhere well when applied over rusted or corroded surfaces.
3. Allow galvanized steel, such as that used for roof gutters, to weather for about six months before painting. If earlier painting is necessary, wash the surface with mineral spirits or VM & P (Varnish Makers & Painters) naphtha, then apply a primer recommended specifically for galvanized surfaces.

BEFORE YOU PAINT EXTERIORS

Check the weather. You can easily ruin a paint job if you forget to consider the weather. Excessive humidity or extremely cold weather can cause you trouble. Good ventilation, regardless of the weather, is essential. Specifically:

1. Unless you are using latex paint, you should not paint on damp days. Moisture on the painting surface may prevent a good bond.
2. If humidity is high, check the surface before painting. If you can feel a film of moisture on the surface, it would be better to wait for a better day. If you are painting inside and the area is air-conditioned, however, neither rain nor humidity will affect the job.
3. Exterior painting is not recommended if the temperature is below 50° F or above 95° F because you may not be able to get a good bond. This is especially critical if you are using latex paint.

If conditions are borderline, good ventilation will help paint to dry. Allow more drying time in damp or humid weather. The label on the can will tell you the normal drying time, but test each coat by touch before you add another. When paint is thoroughly dry, it is firm to the touch and is not sticky.

PAINTING INTERIOR SURFACES

Interior painting and exterior painting are similar in some ways but different in others. Because of the differences, the two types of painting will be treated in separate sections. Some repetition will be unavoidable, but it will be kept to a minimum.

Priming

Previously painted surfaces usually do not require primer coats except where the old paint is worn through or the surface has been damaged.

Wood Surfaces

1. Unpainted wood to be finished with enamel or oil-base paint should be primed with enamel undercoat to seal the wood and provide a better surface. If the unpainted wood is not primed, the enamel coat may be uneven.
2. Unpainted wood to be finished with latex should first be undercoated. Water-thinned paint could raise the grain of the bare wood and leave a rough surface.

If clear finishes are used—Softwoods such as pine, poplar, and gum usually require a sealer for controlling the penetration of the finished coats. In using stain, a sealer is sometimes applied first in order to obtain a lighter, more uniform color. Open-grain hardwoods such as oak, walnut, and mahogany require a paste wood filler, followed by a clear wood sealer. Close grain hardwoods such as maple and birch do not require a filler. The first coat may be a thinned version of the finishing varnish, shellac, or lacquer.

Fig. 9. Polyurethane dries in an hour. It is good on unpainted wood. Courtesy of United Gilsonite.

Masonry Surfaces

Smooth, unpainted masonry surfaces and plaster or plasterboard can be primed with latex paint or latex primer-sealer. The color of the first coat should be similar to the finish coat. Coarse, rough or porous masonry surfaces, such as cement block, cinder block, and concrete, cannot be filled and covered satisfactorily with regular paints. Block filler should be used as a first coat to obtain a smooth sealed surface over which almost any paint can be used.

1. Unpainted brick, while porous, is not as rough as cinder block and similar surfaces and can be primed with latex primer-sealer or with an exterior-type latex paint.
2. Enamel undercoat should be applied over the primer where the finish coat is to be a gloss or semigloss enamel.
3. Follow carefully the manufacturer's label instructions for painting masonry surfaces.

Metal Surfaces

1. Unpainted surfaces should be primed for protection against corrosion and to provide a base for the finish paint. Interior paints do not usually adhere well to bare metal surfaces, and provide little corrosion resistance by themselves.
2. Prime paints for bare metal surfaces must be selected according to the type of metal to be painted. Some primers are made especially for iron or steel; others are for galvanized steel, aluminum, and copper.
3. An enamel undercoat should be used as a second primer if the metal surface is to be finished with enamel; that is, apply the primer first, then the undercoat, and finally the enamel finish. Most enamel undercoats need a light sanding before the topcoat is applied.

Paints for Light Wear Areas

1. Latex interior paints are generally used for areas where there is little need for periodic washing and scrubbing, for example, living rooms, dining rooms, bedrooms, and closets.
2. Interior flat latex paints are used for interior walls and ceilings since they cover well, are easy to apply, dry quickly, are almost ordorless, and can be quickly and easily removed from applicators.
3. Latex paints may be applied directly over semigloss and gloss enamel if the surface is first roughened with sandpaper or liquid sandpaper. If the latter is used, follow carefully the instructions on the container label.
4. Flat alkyd paints are often preferred for wood, drywall and metal surfaces because they are more resistant to damage; also, they can be applied in thicker films to produce a more

uniform appearance. They wash better than interior latex paints and are nearly odorless.

Paints for Heavy Wear Areas

1. Enamels, including latex enamels, are usually preferred for kitchen, bathroom, laundry room, and similar work areas because they withstand intensive cleaning and wear. They form especially hard films, ranging from flat to full gloss.

2. Fast-drying polyurethane enamels and clear varnishes provide excellent hard, flexible finishes for wood floors. Other enamels and clear finishes can also be used, but unless specifically recommended for floors they may be too soft and slower drying, or too hard and brittle.

3. Polyurethane and epoxy enamels are also excellent for concrete floors. For a smooth finish, rough concrete should be properly primed with an alkali-resistant primer to fill the pores. When using these enamels, adequate ventilation is essential for protection from flammable vapors.

Clear Finishes for Wood

1. Varnishes form durable and attractive finishes for interior wood surfaces such as wood paneling, trim, floors, and unpainted furniture. They seal the wood, forming tough, transparent films that will withstand frequent scrubbing and hard use, and are available in flat, semigloss, or satin and gloss finishes.

2. Most varnishes are easily scratched, and the marks are difficult to conceal without redoing the entire surface. A good paste wax applied over the finished varnish— especially on wood furniture—will provide some protection against scratches.

3. Polyurethane and epoxy varnishes are notable for durability and high resistance to stains, abrasions, acids and alkalis, alcohol and chemicals. Adequate ventilation should be provided as protection from flammable vapors when these varnishes are being applied.

4. Shellac and lacquer have uses similar to most varnishes, and these finishes are easy to repair or recoat. They apply easily, dry fast, and are also useful as a sealer and clear

finish under varnish for wood surfaces. The first coat should be thinned as recommended on the container, then sanded very lightly and finished with one or more undiluted coats. Two coats will give a fair sheen, and three a high gloss.

PAINTING EXTERIOR SURFACES

The durability of an exterior paint job depends greatly on surface preparation, the quality of paint selected, the skill of application, the proper spacing of repaintings, the protection of surfaces from the sun and rain, and climatic and local weather conditions.

As previously indicated, conditions must be right for exterior painting. The temperature should not be much below 50° or above 95° F, and surfaces must be free of moisture. Latex paints can be used, however, even if the surface is not bone dry. The best time for exterior painting is after the morning dew has evaporated.

Before you start on the job, make a thorough inspection tour and check the surface condition of window and door frames and surrounding areas, bases of columns of porches and entranceways, steps, siding, downspouts, under-eave areas, and anywhere that moisture is likely to collect.

Priming Wood

1. The tendency of wood to expand and contract during changes in temperature and humidity makes it imperative that a good wood primer be applied to provide the necessary anchorage for the finish paint.
2. Surfaces such as wood siding, porches, trim, shutters, sash doors, and windowsills should be primed with an exterior primer intended for wood. Application should be by brush; surfaces should be thoroughly dry.
3. Painted wood usually does not need priming unless the old paint has cracked, blistered, or peeled. Defective paint must be removed by scraping or wire brushing—preferably down to the bare wood—and then primed.
4. Scratches, dents, recesses, and raw edges should be

smoothed and then touched up with a suitable exterior primer.

Priming Masonry

1. New masonry surfaces should be primed with an exterior latex paint, preferably one specifically made for masonry.
2. Common brick is sometimes sealed with a penetrating type of clear exterior varnish to control efflorescence and spalling (flaking or chipping of the brick). This varnish withstands weather yet allows the natural appearance of the surface to show through.
3. Coarse, rough, and porous surfaces should be covered with a fill coat (block filler), applied by brush to thoroughly penetrate and fill the pores.
4. Old painted surfaces that have become a little chalky should be painted with an exterior oil primer to rebind the chalk. If there is much chalk, it should be removed with a stiff brush or by washing with household washing soda or TSP (trisodium phosphate) mixed with water.

Priming Metal

1. Copper should be cleaned with a phosphoric acid cleaner, buffed and polished until bright, and then coated before it discolors. Copper gutters and downspouts do not require painting. The protective oxide that forms on the copper surface darkens it or turns it green, but does not shorten the life of the metal. Copper is often painted to prevent staining of adjacent painted surfaces.
2. Zinc chromate type primers are effective on copper, aluminum and steel surfaces, but other types are also available for use on metal.
3. Galvanized steel surfaces, such as gutters and downspouts, should be primed with recommended special primers since conventional primers usually do not adhere well to this type of metal. A zinc-dust zinc-oxide primer works well on galvanized steel. Exterior latex paints, but not oil paints, are sometimes used directly over galvanized surfaces.
4. Unpainted iron and steel surfaces rust when exposed to the weather. Rust, dirt, oils, and old loose paint should be re-

moved from these surfaces by wire brushing or power-tool cleaning. The surface should then be treated with an anti-corrosive primer.

Finishing

1. All exterior surfaces, properly primed or previously painted, can be finished with either exterior oil paint or exterior latex paint.
2. Latex paints are easy to apply, have good color retention, and can be used on slightly damp surfaces.
3. Oil- or alkyd-base paints have excellent penetrating properties. They provide good adhesion, durability, and resistance to abrasion and blistering on wood and other porous surfaces.
4. Mildew, fungus, and mold growths on exterior surfaces are a problem in areas where high temperature and humidity are prevalent. Use paint that contains agents to resist bacterial and mold growth.
5. Colored exterior house paints must resist chalking so that colors will not fade and erosion of the paint film will be minimized. The manufacturer's label will indicate whether the paint is a nonchalking type. Some white exterior house paints are expected to chalk slightly as a means of self-cleaning.

WORKING WITH COLOR

The average paint store has paint-mixing machines where, at least theoretically, they can match any color you bring into the store. I say "theoretically" because it is not really true. Different surfaces absorb paints to varying degrees, so no matter how close the paint dealer can get, the paint will never be exactly the shade that you wish.

At any rate, buying paint custom-mixed like this is expensive. It is better for the painter to know how to mix colors. You can get exactly the shade you need, and for only the price of the colorant.

Colorant for the job can be universal tinting colors. These are so named because they are good for both latex and oil-base paints. They come in tubes for small jobs, and in cans if you expect to use the particular color frequently.

Fig. 10. Tinting colors can create any color you wish. Courtesy of Benjamin Moore.

When using colors, the following tips should be useful:

1. Add the color to the paint gradually, mixing it in thoroughly.
2. The colorant will mix in more readily if it is first mixed with a tiny bit of thinner.
3. Try the mixed paint on a spot where it is in full light. Shadows can create false readings.
4. Let the paint dry before determining its exact shade.
5. Do not add more colorant than specified on the container.

COLORS

The diagram shown in Fig. 11 shows the three primary colors, their secondaries, and what may be called tertiary colors. Opposite each of these there has been placed one of the notes of the chromatic music scale forming a perfect octave. It is interesting to note that the claim has been made, and with much insistence, that any scheme of color that may be selected and which may be struck as a chord will, if the chord is harmonious, become a harmonious scheme of color. If this chord produces a discord of music, there will be a discord of color.

By definition, primary colors are those that cannot be made by

279

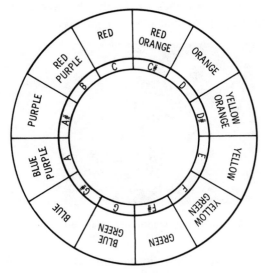

Fig. 11. Illustrating the three primary colors with the
secondaries and tertiary colors shown.

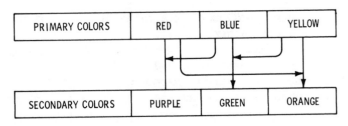

Fig. 12. A diagram of primary and secondary colors.

mixing two or more colors together. The three primary colors
are, *red, blue,* and *yellow.* Fig. 12 shows a diagram of the primary and secondary colors. The colors obtained from mixing
any two of the primary colors together are called secondary
colors. There are three secondary colors—*purple, green* and
orange.

Red and blue gives *purple*
Blue and yellow gives *green*
Red and yellow gives *orange*

By mixing any two of the secondary colors together you get what are called tertiary colors, which are: *citrine, olive,* and *russet*.

Orange and green gives *citrine*
Green and purple gives *olive*
Orange and purple gives *russet*

Black and white are not regarded as colors. A good black can be produced by mixing the three primary colors together in proper proportions. By adding white to any color you produce a tint of that color. By adding black to any color you get a shade of that color. That is the difference between *tint* and *shade*. The use of black subdues or lowers the tone of any color to which it is added. To preserve the richness of colors when you wish to darken them, use the primary colors instead of black. To make a yellow darker, use red or blue, and to darken blue, add red and yellow, and so on.

Every shade or tint of color required by the painter can be made from red, blue, and yellow with black and white. To make any of the umbers or siennas lighter in color and to preserve the clear richness of tone, always use lemon chrome instead of white. If you wish a subdued or muddy umber or sienna color, then use white.

The most useful primary colors are:

Yellows—*lemon chrome, deep ocher*
Reds—*vermilion, Venetian red, crimson lake*
Blues—*Prussian blue, ultramarine*

Gold or silver leaf harmonizes with all colors and, with black and white in small quantities, can be used to bring into harmony the most glaring colors. The old-time heraldic painters knew the value of outlining their strong primary colors with gold, silver, black, or white to bring them into harmony with each other. The Egyptians and other ancient people made use of the same knowledge in their decorative schemes. Yellow ocher is a useful color. In its pure state it is admirable for large wall spaces, and if you are in doubt as to what color to use to complete a color scheme, you will find ocher or one of its shades or tints will supply the missing link.

Red on walls makes a room look smaller and will absorb light. Yellow gives light and airiness to any room and it will also reflect light. Useful colors in large quantities for churches, public halls, etc., are:

Primrose red
Terra cotta (white, burnt sienna, lemon chrome)
All tints of ocher
Flesh colors (white and burnt sienna)
Pea green, apple green
Gray green (white, paris green and a touch of black)
Ivory shades (white, lemon chrome, or ocher)
Old rose (white, ocher, Venetian red, or pure Indian red and black)
Nile blue and Nile green (white, Prussian blue, lemon chrome)
Light citrine, light olive, light russet

For ceilings the best tints are the creams and ivory tints, and gray. Creams and ivory tints are made from white tint with one or more of these colors.

Lemon chrome
Orange chrome
Ocher
Raw sienna

To produce a warm tone, add a small quantity of burnt sienna, vermilion, or Venetian red. To produce a colder tone, use a little green, black, raw umber, or blue. Grays are made from white tint with either black, black and green, blue and umber, black and red, red and blue, or burnt sienna and blue. Light colors are used for ceilings in preference to dark colors. Contrasting colors are better for ceilings than a lighter tint of the wall color.

PAINT FAILURES

There are a number of reasons for exterior paint failures. One of the major causes of paint failure is moisture. Quality of paint and the method of application are others.

1. If steel nails have been used for the application of the siding, disfiguring rust spots may occur at the nailheads, particularly where they are exposed. Spotting is somewhat less apparent where steel nails have been set and puttied. Similarly, the spotting may be minimized, in the case of flush nailing, by setting the nailheads below the surface and puttying. The puttying should be preceded by a priming coat.

2. Brick and other types of masonry are not always waterproof, and continued rains may result in a damp interior wall or wet spots where water has worked through. If this trouble persists, it may be well to use a waterproof coating on the exposed surface. Transparent coatings can be obtained for this purpose.

3. Calking is usually required where a change in material occurs, such as that of wood siding abutting against brick chimneys or walls. The wood should always have a prime coating of paint for proper adhesion of the calking compound. Calking guns with cartridges can be obtained and are the best means of waterproofing these joints.

4. Rain water flowing down over wood siding may work through butts and end joints and sometimes may work up under the butt edge by capillary action. Setting the butt end joints in white lead is an old-time custom that is very effective in preventing water from entering. Painting under the butt edges at the lap adds mechanical resistance to water ingress. Moisture changes in the siding cause some swelling and shrinking that may break the paint film. Treating the siding with a water repellent before it is applied is an effective method of reducing capillary action. For houses already built, the water repellent could be applied under the butt edges of bevel siding or along the joints of drop siding and at all vertical joints. Excess repellent on the face of painted surfaces should be wiped off.

5. Two of the most common paint problems are peeling and bleeding. Peeling usually has to do with moisture, though incompatibility of paints also causes it. At any rate, check for moisture penetration, and check paint compatibility. All peeling paint must come off before painting. Bleeding is

Fig. 13. Bleeding.

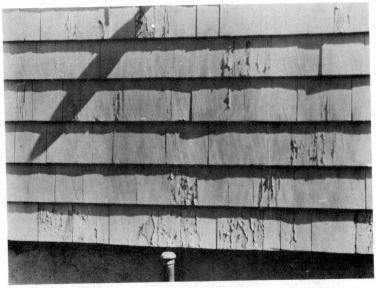

Fig. 14. Peeling.

also sometimes due to paint incompatibility or, on interiors, it can occur if you apply flat paint over plaster. It can also occur when the paint used is too thin, or when flat paint is applied over enamel. Check these situations out before painting.

SUMMARY

Painting appears to be a simple operation, but it takes concentration and the use of proper tools and techniques to do a good job.

You can normally use either a brush or roller though in some instances, such as when painting a highly textured surface, only a brush will serve well. Take care and pick quality brushes and rollers and take good care of the tools—clean them well after use and store properly.

A paint sprayer may also be used, but the paint must be of the proper consistency. Make sure surrounding areas are covered. Before using any kind of paint in any application read the label and follow the manufacturer's directions.

If two or more coats are required the surfaces are first prepared and primed. This is as important—even more important—than applying the finish coat.

Working with color is also an important aspect of painting. Colors may be mixed from scratch (white with color added), store bought, or bought ready tinted.

Problems are also a part of painting, and water is the chief culprit. All potential problems must be cleared up before painting begins.

REVIEW QUESTIONS

1. What are the common tools used for painting?
2. What are typical preparation jobs?
3. What is the chief problem when paint problems occur?
4. When is spray painting a good idea?
5. What is creating color from "scratch"?

CHAPTER 21

Checklist for Maintenance and Repair

A house that is well constructed, with adequate attention to construction details and to the choice of materials used to build the house, will need far less maintenance than one that is not well built. It is indeed discouraging to the houseowner to begin repair and maintenance almost before he has moved in! An extra $40 used for rust-resistant nails on the siding, for example, may save $500 by requiring less frequent painting.

What follows are conditions and areas to check for problems, and how to solve them.

BASEMENT

The basement may sometimes be damp for several months after the house has been built. In most cases, this moisture comes from masonry walls and floors and will progressively disappear. In cases of persistent dampness, however, the owner should check various areas in order to eliminate any possibilities for water entry.

The following areas may be the source for some of the trouble caused by the entry of moisture:

1. Check the drainage at the downspouts. The final grade around the house should be away from the building, and a splash block should be provided to drain water away from the foundation wall.

2. Some settling of the soil may occur at the foundation wall and form water pockets. These areas should be filled and tamped so that surface water can drain away.

3. Some leaking may occur in a poured concrete wall at the tie wires. These usually seal themselves, but larger holes should be filled with a cement mortar. Clean and slightly dampen the area first for good adhesion.

4. Concrete block or other masonry walls exposed above grade often show dampness on the interior after a prolonged rainy spell. There are concrete paints on the market that increase the resistance to moisture seepage. Waterproofing materials may also be used on the exterior walls.

5. Moisture absorption. There should be at least a 6-inch clearance between the bottom of the siding and the finish grade to prevent moisture absorption. Shrubs and foundation plantings should also be kept away from the wall to improve circulation and drying. In lawn sprinkling, do not allow the water to spray against the walls of the house.

6. Check areas between the foundation wall and the sill. Any openings should be filled with calk. This filling will decrease heat loss and also prevent entry of insects into the basement.

7. Dampness in the basement in the early summer months is often augmented by opening the windows for ventilation during the day. This will allow warm, moisture-laden outside air to enter. The lower temperature of the basement will cool the incoming air and frequently cause condensation to collect and drip from cold-water pipes and also collect on colder parts of the masonry walls and floors. To air out the basement, open the windows during the night.

In aggravated cases, heating the basement to raise the temperature 5 to 10 degrees, with the windows closed, has proved helpful. Heating lowers the humidity, warms the cold masonry, and dries up the moisture. On cool days no heat is required, and the windows may be opened. As the summer advances and the masonry warms up, condensation will not usually occur on the walls but may occur on the cold-water pipes. Wrapping such pipes has proved helpful in reducing condensation and drip.

A desiccant, such as calcium chloride, is sometimes used to lower the humidity in basements. Dehumidifiers are also available in a variety of sizes. Such units are generally enclosed in a cabinet and are operated by electricity. The doors and windows should be closed at all times during dehumidification; otherwise the moisture in the entering air will continually replace the moisture extracted by the desiccant or dehumidifier.

CRAWL-SPACE AREA

The crawl-space area should be checked as follows:

1. If the house is located in a termite area, be sure to make annual inspections, preferably in the late spring or early summer, for termite activity or damage. These inspections are a must if the house or a part of the house is built over a crawl space. Termite tubes on the walls or piers are an indication of their activity. A well-constructed house will have a termite shield under the wood sill with a 2-inch extension on the interior. Examine the shield for proper projection, and also any cracks in the foundation walls, as these cracks form good channels for termites to enter.

2. While in this crawl space, it is well to check the area for any decay that may be occurring in the girders or joists, as well as for signs of condensation on wood members of the floor framing. Use a penknife to test questionable areas for rot and decay. There are products, such as Git Rot for repairing rotted wood. This is available at marine supply stores.

3. If the crawl space seems damp and the ground moist, it may be due to lack of proper ventilation. The crawl-space ventilators should be of adequate size and should be so located that there is cross circulation. The use of a soil cover, 55-pound saturated felt or heavier, or polyethylene sheeting, on the ground of the crawl space will prevent much of the soil moisture from entering the area.

ROOF AND ATTIC

The roof and attic should be checked as indicated.

1. If there are a few humps on asphalt-shingle tabs, they most likely are due to nails that have not been driven into solid wood. Remove such nails and replace with others driven into sound wood. There may be a line of buckled shingles along the roof. This ordinarily is caused by applying the shingles to roof boards that are not dry and to roof sheathing that varies in thickness. The shrinkage of the wood in the wide boards between the nails will also cause these humps by buckling the shingles. Time and hot weather tend to reduce this condition.

2. A dirt streak down the gable end of the house is often caused by rain entering the rake molding from shingles that have insufficient projection. A cant strip would ordinarily have prevented this situation.

3. In winters of heavy snows, ice dams may form at the eaves, and these often result in water entering the cornice and walls of the house. The immediate remedy is to remove the snow on the roof for a short distance above the gutters and, if necessary, in the valleys. Additional insulation between heated rooms and roof space, and increased ventilation, will help to decrease the melting of snow on the roof and thus minimize formation of ice at the gutters and in the valleys. Deep snow in valleys also sometimes forms ice dams that cause water to back up under shingles and valley flashing. You can also get heating cables to install in gutters.

4. Roof leaks are often caused by improper flashing at the valley, ridge, or around the chimney. Observe these areas during a rainy spell to discover the source. Water may travel many feet from the point of entry before it drips off the roof members.

5. The attic ventilators serve two important purposes—that of summer ventilation as a means of lowering the attic temperature to improve comfort conditions in the rooms below and that of winter ventilation to remove moisture that may work through the ceiling and condense in the attic space. The ventilators should be open both winter and summer.

In order to check for sufficient ventilating area during cold weather, examine the attic after a prolonged cold period. If nails protruding from the roof are heavily coated with frost, it is evident that ventilation is not sufficient. Frost may also collect on the roof sheathing, first appearing near the eaves on the north side of the roof. Increase the size of the ventilators or place additional ones in the protected underside of the cornice. This will improve air movement and circulation.

EXTERIOR WALLS

One of the major problems in maintenance of a wood-covered house is the exterior paint finish. There are a number of reasons for paint failures, many of them known, others not as yet thoroughly investigated. One of the major causes of paint failure is moisture in its various forms. Quality of paint and method of application are other reasons. Correct methods of application, types of paint, and the problems encountered are covered in Chapter 20, on Painting.

Another problem with exterior walls that the owner may encounter in his house are that if steel nails have been used for the application of the siding, rust spots may occur at the nailhead. Such rust spots are quite common where nails are driven flush with the heads exposed. Spotting is somewhat less apparent where steel nails have been set and puttied. The spotting may be minimized, in the case of flush nailing, by setting the nailhead below the surface and puttying. The puttying should be preceded by a priming coat. Take care of these nails just before the house requires repainting.

Brick and other types of masonry are not always waterproof, and continued rains may result in damp interior walls or wet spots where water has soaked through. If this trouble persists, it may be well to use a waterproof coating over the exposed surfaces. Coatings can be obtained for this purpose. Calking is usually required where a change in materials occurs, such as that of wood siding abutting against brick chimneys or walls. The wood should always have a prime coating of paint for proper adhesion of the calking compound. Calking guns with cartridges can be obtained and are the best means of waterproofing these joints.

Rain water flowing down over wood siding may work through

butt and end joints and sometimes may work up under the butt edge by capillary action. Coating edges with paint helps, and painting under the butt edges at the lap adds mechanical resistance to water intrusion. However, moisture changes in the siding cause some swelling and shrinking that may break the paint film. Treating the siding with a water repellent before it is applied is an effective method of reducing capillary action. For houses already built, the water repellent could be applied under the butt edges of bevel siding or along the joints of drop siding and at all vertical joints. Excess repellent on the face of painted surfaces should be wiped off.

INTERIOR WALLS

In a newly constructed house, many small plaster cracks may develop during or after the first heating season. These cracks are usually due to the drying and shrinking of the structural members. For this reason, it is advisable to wait for a part of the heating season before painting, if the walls are plastered. These cracks can then be filled before painting. Because of the curing period ordinarily required for plastered walls, it is not advisable to apply oil-base paints until at least 60 days after plastering is completed. Latex paints can be applied without waiting.

Large plaster cracks often indicate a structural weakness in the framing. One of the common areas that may need correction is around a basement stairway. Framing may not be adequate for the loads of the walls and ceilings. In such cases, the use of an additional post and pedestal may be required to correct this fault. Inadequate framing around fireplaces and chimney openings, and joists that are not doubled under partitions, are other common sources of weakness.

Moisture on Windows

Points to be noted with respect to moisture on windows are as follows:

1. During cold weather, condensation, and in cold climates, frost will collect on the inner face of single-glazed windows. Water from the condensation or melting frost runs

down the glass and soaks into the wood sash to cause stain, decay, and paint failure. The water may rust steel sash. To prevent such condensation, the window should be provided with a storm sash. Double glazing will also minimize this condensation.

2. Occasionally, in very cold weather, frost may form on the inner surfaces of the storm windows. This may be caused by:

   a. Loose-fitting window sash that allows moisture to enter the space between the window and storm sash.

   b. High relative humidity in the living quarters.

Generally, the condensation on storm sash does not create a maintenance problem, but it may be a nuisance. Weatherstripping the inner sash offers increased resistance to moisture flow and may prevent this condensation. Lower relative humidities in the house are also helpful.

Moisture on Doors

Condensation may collect on single exterior doors during severe cold periods for the same reasons as described for windows. Here again, the water may cause damage to the door and to the finish. Storm doors offer the most practical means of preventing or minimizing such condensation. The addition of storm doors will also decrease the warping of the exterior doors.

FLOORS

A finish floor that has been improperly laid is a source of trouble for the housewife. This flooring may have been laid with varying moisture contents in the boards or at too high a moisture content. Cracks or openings in the floor appear during the heating season as the flooring dries out. If the floor has a few large cracks, one expedient is to fit matching strips of wood between the flooring strips and to glue them in place. In severe cases, it may be necessary to replace sections of the floor or to refloor the entire house. Another method would be to cover the existing flooring with a thin flooring, $5/16$ or $3/8$ inch thick. This would require removal of the base shoe, fitting the thin flooring around door jambs, and perhaps sawing off the door bottoms.

SUMMARY

Preventive maintenance, and alertness to problems, will often prevent a major repair bill. A damp basement will sometimes occur for several months after a house has been completed, and in most cases it will progressively disappear. In cases of persistent dampness, the owner should check various areas in order to eliminate this problem. Checking drainage downspouts for proper grade to carry away drain water is one of the first on the list. Some settling of the soil may occur at the foundation wall and form a water pocket.

If a house is designed with a crawl-space area, it should be checked for termite activity or damage. A well-constructed house will have a termite shield under the wood sill; this should also be checked for proper projection. Crawl-space ventilators should be checked for proper air circulation, as well as any obstruction which could prevent circulation.

The roof and attic should be inspected for humps in the asphalt shingles; these are an indication of loose nails. All flashing around chimneys, valleys, and ridges should be checked for possible leaks. Attics should be checked for proper ventilation and leaks in the roof.

Interior and exterior walls should be checked periodically for cracks, paint peeling, and air leaks. Windows should be checked for air leaks and freedom of operation. Floors should be checked for cracks or openings which appear during the heating season. Floor joists should be checked for cracks or decay.

REVIEW QUESTIONS

1. How often should a frame house be painted?
2. Why does plaster crack above windows and door openings?
3. How can dampness be corrected in a crawl space?
4. What should be checked when inspecting a roof?
5. Why does a wood floor crack or buckle after being installed?

CHAPTER 22

Physical Characteristics of Wood

Wood, like all plant material, is made up of cells, or fibers, which when magnified have an appearance similar to, though less regular than, that of the common honeycomb. The walls of the honeycomb correspond to the walls of the fibers, and the cavities in the honeycomb correspond to the hollow or open spaces of the fibers.

SOFTWOODS AND HARDWOODS

All lumber is divided as a matter of convenience into two great groups: softwoods and hardwoods. The softwoods in general are the coniferous or cone-bearing trees, such as the various pines, spruces, hemlocks, firs, and cedar. The hardwoods are the noncone-bearing trees, such as the maple, oak, poplar, and the like. These terms are used as a matter of custom, for not all so-called softwoods are soft nor are all so-called hardwoods necessarily hard. As a matter of fact, such so-called softwoods as long-leaf southern pine and Douglas fir are much harder than poplar, basswood, etc., which are called hardwoods.

Other and perhaps more accurate terms often used for these two groups are the needle-bearing trees and the broad-leaved trees, referring to the softwoods and hardwoods, respectively. In general, the softwoods are more commonly used for structural purposes such as for joists, studs, girders, and posts, while the hardwoods are more likely to be used for interior finish, flooring, and furniture. The softwoods are also used for interior finish and in many cases for floors, but are not often used for furniture.

MOISTURE CONTENT

While the tree is living, both the cells and cell walls are filled with water to an extent. As soon as the tree is cut, the water within the cells, or "free water" as it is called, begins to evaporate. This process continues until practically all of the "free water" has left the wood. When this stage is reached the wood is said to be at the fiber-saturation point; that is, what water is contained is mainly in the cell or fiber walls.

Except in a few species, there is no change in size during this preliminary drying process, and therefore no shrinkage during the evaporation of the "free water." Shrinkage begins only when water begins to leave the cell walls themselves. What causes shrinkage and other changes in wood is not fully understood; but it is thought that as water leaves the cell walls, they contract, becoming harder and denser, thereby causing a general reduction in size of the piece of wood. If the specimen is placed in an oven which is maintained at 212° F, the temperature of boiling water, the water will evaporate and the specimen will continue to lose weight for a time. Finally a point is reached at which the weight remains substantially constant. This is another way of saying that all of the water in the cells and cell walls has been driven off. The piece is then said to be "oven dry."

If it is now taken out of the oven and allowed to remain in the open air, it will gradually take on weight, due to the absorption of moisture from the air. As when placed in the oven, a point is reached at which the weight of the wood in contact with the air remains more or less constant. Careful tests, however, show that it does not remain exactly constant, it will take on and give off water as the moisture in the atmosphere increases or decreases. Thus, a piece of wood will contain more water during the humid, moist summer months than in the colder, drier winter months. When the piece is in this condition it is in "equilibrium with the air" and is said to be "air dry."

A piece of lumber cut from a green tree and left in the atmosphere in such a way that the air may circulate freely about it will gradually arrive at this air-dry condition. This ordinarily takes from one to three months, and the process is termed "air seasoning." It can be greatly hastened by placing the wood in an artificially heated oven or "dry kiln" until the moisture content of the wood is that of air dryness. The amount of water contained by wood in the green condition varies greatly, not only with the species but in the same species, and even in the same tree, according to the position in the tree. But as a general average, at the fiber-saturation point, most woods contain from 23 to 30 percent water as compared with the oven-dry weight of the wood. When air dry, most woods contain from 12 to 15 percent moisture.

SHRINKAGE

As the wood dries from the green state, which is that of the freshly cut tree, to the fiber-saturation point, except in a few species, there is no change other than that of weight. It has already been pointed out that as the moisture dries out of the cell walls, in addition to the decrease in weight, shrinkage results in a definite decrease in size. It has been found, however, that there is little or no decrease along the length of the grain, and that the decrease is at right angles to the grain.

This is an important consideration to be remembered when framing a building. For example, a stud in a wall will not shrink appreciably in length, whereas it will shrink somewhat in both the 2-inch and the 4-inch way. In like manner, a joist, if it is green when put in place, will change in depth as it seasons in the building. This shrinkage is illustrated in Fig. 1. These principles of shrinkage also explain why an edge-grain or quarter-sawed floor is less likely to open up than a flat-grain floor.

DENSITY

The tree undergoes a considerable impetus early every spring and grows very rapidly for a short time. Large amounts of water are carried through the cells to the rapidly growing branches and leaves at the top of the tree. This water passes upward mainly in

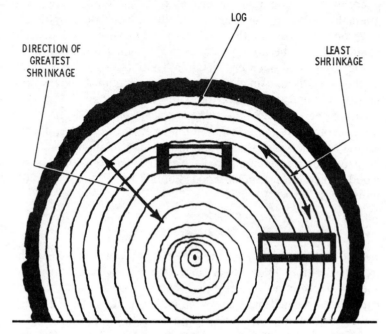

Fig. 1. Illustrating the shrinkage of wood from end to end.

the outer layers of the tree. The result is that the cells next to the bark, which are formed during the period of rapid growth, have thin walls and large passages. Later on, during the summer, the rate of growth slows up and the demand for water is less. The cells which are formed during the summer have much thicker walls and much smaller pores. Thus, a year's growth forms two types of wood—the spring wood, as it is called, being characterized by softness and openness of grain, and the summer wood by hardness and closeness, or density, of grain. The spring wood and summer wood growth for one year is called an "annual ring."

There is one ring for each year of growth. This development of spring wood and summer wood is a marked characteristic of practically all woods and is clearly evident in such trees as the yellow pines and firs, and less so in the white pines, maple, and the like. Careful examination will reveal this annual ring, however, in practically all species. It follows, therefore, that a tree in which the dense summer wood predominates is stronger than one in which the soft spring wood predominates. This is a point which should be borne in mind in selecting material for important members such as girders and posts carrying heavy loads. The strength of wood of the same species varies markedly with the density. For example, Douglas fir or southern pine, carefully selected for density, is one-sixth stronger than lumber of the same species and knot limitations in which the spring wood predominates. Trees having approximately one-third or more of cross-sectional area in summer wood fulfill one of the requirements for structural timbers.

ESTIMATING DENSITY

It must be remembered that the small cells or fibers which make up the wood structure are hollow. Wood substance itself has a specific gravity of about 1.5, and therefore will sink in water. It is stated that wood substance of all species is practically of the same density. Strength of wood depends upon its density and varies with its density. The actual dry weight of lumber is a good criterion of its strength, although weight can not always be relied upon as a basis for determining strength, as other important factors frequently must be considered in a specific piece of wood.

The hardness of wood is also another factor which assists in estimating the strength of wood. A test sometimes used is cutting across the grain. This test cannot be utilized in the commercial grading of lumber because a moisture content will affect the hardness and because hardness thus measured cannot be adequately defined. The annual rings found in practically all species are an important consideration in estimating density, although the annual rings indicate different conditions in different species. In ring-porous hardwoods and in the conifers, where the contrast between spring wood and summer wood is definite, the proportion of hard summer wood is an indication of the strength of the individual piece of wood. The amount of summer wood, however, cannot always be relied upon as an indication of strength, because summer wood itself varies in density. When cut across the grain with a knife, the density of summer wood may be estimated on the basis of hardness, color, and luster.

In conifers, annual rings of average width indicate denser material or a larger proportion of summer wood than in wood with either wide or narrow rings. In some old conifers of virgin growth, in which the more recent annual rings are narrow, the wood is less dense than where there has been normal growth. On the other hand, in young trees where the growth has not been impeded by other trees, the rings are wider and in consequence the wood less dense. These facts may account for the belief that all second-growth timber and all sapwood are weak. In accepting wood for density, the contrast between summer wood and spring wood should be pronounced.

Oak, ash, hickory, and other ring-porous hardwoods in general rank high in strength when the annual rings are wide. In this respect they contrast with conifers. These species have more summer wood than spring wood as the rings become wider. For this reason, oak, hickory, ash, and elm of second growth are considered superior because of fast growth and increase in proportion of summer wood. These conditions do not always exist, however, for exceptions occur, especially in ash and oak, where, although the summer wood is about normal, it may not be dense or strong. Very narrow rings in ring-porous hardwoods are likely to indicate weak and brashy material composed largely of spring wood with big pores. Maple, birch, beech, and other diffuse-porous hardwoods in general show no definite relationship between the width of rings and density, except that usually narrow rings indicate brash wood.

STRENGTH

Wood, when used in ordinary structures, is called upon to have three types of strength—tension, compression, and shear.

Tension

Tension is the technical term for a pulling stress. For example, if two men are having a tug of war with a rope, the rope is in tension. The tensile strength of wood, especially of the structural grades, is very high.

Compression

If, however, the men at opposite ends of a 2 × 4 are trying to push each other over, the timber is in compression. Tension and compression represent, therefore, exactly opposite forces.

Shear

Shear is harder to explain. If two or three planks are placed one upon the other between two blocks, and a person were to stand in the middle, the planks would bend and assume a position similar to that shown in Fig. 2. It will be noted that at the outer ends the boards tend to slip past each other.

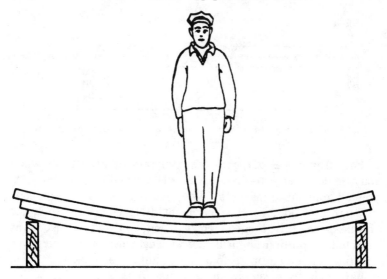

Fig. 2. Illustrating shear in lumber.

If the planks were securely spiked through from top to bottom, the slipping would be in a great measure prevented and the boards would act more as one piece of wood. In very solid timber there is the same tendency for the various parts of the piece to slip past each other. This tendency is called *horizontal shear*. A defect, such as a check, which runs horizontally through a piece of a timber and tends to separate the upper from the lower part, is a weakness in shear.

It is well to analyze this matter a little further. Suppose that the planks were spiked through at the center of span only, i.e., halfway between the blocks. Such spikes would not increase the stiffness of the planks. It is clear, therefore that there is no horizontal shear near the center of the span (Fig. 3), and that the shear increases as one approaches either end of the beam. This will explain why, as most carpenters have doubtless observed, steel stirrups are used in concrete beams (weak in shear), why there is usually none near the center, and why they are put closer and closer together near the ends of the beams.

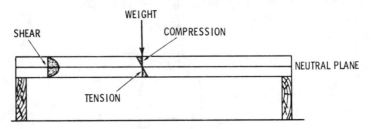

Fig. 3. Illustrating the different proportions of tension, compression, and shear.

For all practical purposes the compressive strength of wood may be considered to equal its tensile strength. It has been extremely difficult to make any direct measurements of the tensile strength of wood. In an experiment designed to ascertain the tensile strength of a specimen of wood, a 4″ × 4″ piece was selected. A portion about a foot in length near the center was carefully cut down on all four sides until it was exactly 3/4 inch square. The test specimen was placed in a machine which gripped the 4″ × 4″ ends securely and a pull was exerted. The specimen did not pull apart. The 3/4-inch-square section held and actually pulled out of the end of the 4″ × 4″, leaving a 3/4-inch-square hole. This is an excellent illustration of how a piece may fail from shear rather than tension, the shear in this case being insufficient to prevent the 3/4-inch-square piece from pulling out.

DEADWOOD

Because in some instances persons are prejudiced against the use of timber cut from dead trees, it is customary for individuals to specify that only timber cut from live trees will be accepted. It is true, however, that when sound trees that are dead are sawed into lumber and the weathered or charred outside is cut away, the resulting lumber cannot be distinguished from that coming from live trees except insofar as the lumber from dead trees may be somewhat seasoned at the time it is sawed. It must be remembered that the heartwood of a living tree is fully matured and that in the sapwood only a small portion of the cells are in a living condition. As a consequence, most of the wood cut from trees is already dead, even when the tree itself is considered alive.

For structural purposes, it may be said that lumber cut from fire- or insect-killed trees is just as good as any other lumber unless the wood has been subjected to further decay or insect attack.

DRY-ROT

Loosely used, the term "dry-rot" is applied to any type of dry crumbly rot and includes under these circumstances all types of brown decay in wood. The pathologist uses the term "dry-rot" in the limited sense as it applies to the work of certain decay fungi which are frequently found growing in timber where they appear to have access to no moisture. Decay fungi will not grow in perfectly dry wood and no material decay need be expected in wood used under shelter and maintained in a normal air-dry condition. With moist wood the fungi are able to penetrate amazingly long distances because they extend their water-supply system by means of slender, minute, porous strands. Fungi of other kinds produce a rot not unlike dry-rot, but brown or yellow in color. The wood in an advanced state is shrunken, and in some places the cracks are filled with a white soggy mass, the wood itself being brittle, friable, and easily crushed into powder.

VIRGIN AND SECOND GROWTH

Occasionally an order calls for lumber of either virgin growth or second growth. The terms, however, are without significance, as an individual cannot tell one type from the other when it is delivered.

The virgin growth, which is also called old growth or first growth, refers to timber that grows in the forest along with many other trees, and therefore has suffered the consequence of the fight for sunlight and moisture.

The second growth is considered as that timber which grows up with less of the competition for sunlight and moisture that characterizes first-growth timber.

Because of environment, the virgin growth is usually thought of as wood of slow-growing type, whereas the second growth is considered as of relatively rapid growth, evidenced by wider annual rings. In such hardwoods as ash, hickory, elm, and oak these wider annual rings are supposed to indicate stronger and tougher wood, whereas in the conifers such as pine and fir, this condition is supposed to result in a weaker and brasher wood. For this reason, where the strength and toughness are desired, the second growth is preferred among hardwoods, and virgin growth is desired in conifers. Because of the variety of conditions under which both virgin and second growth timbers grow, because virgin growth may have the characteristics of second growth, and because second growth may have the characteristics of virgin timber, it is advisable in judging the strength of wood to rely upon its density and rate of growth rather than upon its being either virgin or second growth.

TIME OF CUTTING TIMBER

The time when timber is cut has very little to do with its durability or other desirable properties if, after it is cut, it is cared for properly. Timber cut in the late spring, however, or early summer is more likely to be attacked by insects and fungi. In addition, seasoning will proceed much more rapidly during the summer months and, therefore, will result in checking, unless the lumber is shaded from the intense sunlight. It is stated that there is practically no difference in the moisture content in green lumber, either during the summer or winter.

AIR-DRIED AND KILN-DRIED WOOD

There is a prevailing misapprehension that air-dried lumber is stronger or better than kiln-dried lumber. Exhaustive tests have conclusively shown that good kiln-drying and good air-drying have exactly the same results on the strength of the wood. Wood increases in strength with the elimination of moisture content. This may account for the claim that kiln-dried lumber is stronger than air-dried lumber. This has little significance because in use wood will come to practically the same moisture content whether it has been kiln-dried or air-dried.

The same kiln-drying process cannot be applied to all species of wood. Consequently it must be remembered that lack of certain strength properties in wood may be due to improper kiln-drying. Similar damage also may result from air seasoning under unsuitable conditions.

SAPWOOD VERSUS HEARTWOOD

The belief is common that in some species the heartwood is stronger than the sapwood and that the reverse is the case in such species as hickory and ash. Tests have shown conclusively that neither is the case, and that sapwood is not necessarily stronger than heartwood or heartwood stronger than sapwood, but that density rather than other factors makes the difference in strength. In trees that are mature, the sapwood is frequently weaker, whereas in young trees the sapwood may be stronger. Density, proportion of spring and summer wood, then must be the basis of consideration of strength rather than whether the wood is sapwood or heartwood. Under unfavorable conditions, the sapwood of most species is more subject to decay than the heartwood.

BLUE STAIN

In the sapwood of many species of both softwoods and hardwoods, there often develops a bluish-black discoloration known as blue stain. It does not indicate an early stage of decay, nor does it have any practicable effect on the strength of the wood. Blue stain is caused by a fungus growth in unseasoned lumber. Although objectionable where appearance is of importance, as in unpainted sash or trim, blue stain need cause no concern for framing lumber. Precautions should be taken, however, to make sure that no decay fungus is present with the blue satin.

SUMMARY

Lumber is divided as a matter of convenience into two groups—softwood and hardwood. Softwoods are generally cone-bearing trees such as various pines, spruces, hemlocks, firs, and cedars. Hardwoods are noncone-bearing trees such as maple, oak, and poplar. These terms are used only as a classification and do not mean that so-called softwood is particularly soft, nor that hardwood is particularly hard.

Except for a few species, there is no change in size during the preliminary drying process, and therefore no shrinkage during the evaporation of the free water. There is generally no change in the lumber other than that of weight. There is little or no decrease along the length of the grain—the decrease, if any, will be at right angles to the grain. If green or wet lumber is used in construction, the length will not decrease—it will be the depth and width that will change.

When using wood in ordinary structures, it is called upon to have three types of strength—tension, shear, and compression. Tension is the pulling strength of wood; shear is the strength available at both ends of a piece of timber. Compression is the opposite of tension, whereas tension is the pulling force and compression is the pushing force.

REVIEW QUESTIONS

1. What are tension, compression, and shear of wood?
2. Explain the moisture content of lumber.
3. What is the percentage of shrinkage in drying lumber?
4. What is dry-rot?
5. Explain blue stain in lumber.

Glossary of Housing Terms

Air-Dried Lumber—Lumber that has been piled in yards or sheds for any length of time. For the United States as a whole, the minimum moisture content of thoroughly air-dried lumber is 12 to 15 percent, with the average somewhat higher.

Airway—A space between roof insulation and roof boards for movement of air.

Alligatoring—Coarse checking pattern characterized by a slipping of the new paint coating over the old coating to the extent that the old coating can be seen through the fissures.

Anchor Bolts—Bolts to secure a wooden sill to a concrete or masonry floor, foundation, or wall.

Apron—The flat member of the inside trim of a window placed against the wall immediately beneath the stool.

Areaway—An open subsurface space adjacent to a building used to admit light or air, or as a means of access to a basement or cellar.

Asphalt—Most asphalt is a residue from evaporated petroleum. It is insoluble in water but is soluble in gasoline and melts when heated. Used in making waterproof roof coverings of many types, exterior wall coverings, flooring tile, and the like.

Astragal—A molding, attached to one of a pair of swinging doors, against which the other door strikes.

307

Attic Ventilators—In home building, usually openings in gables or ventilators in the roof. Also, mechanical devices to force ventilation by the use of power-driven fans. Also see *Louver*.

Backband—Molding used on the side of a door or window casing for ornamentation or to increase the width of the trim.

Backfill—The replacement of excavated earth into a pit or trench or against a foundation wall.

Balusters—Small spindles or members forming the main part of a railing for a stairway or balcony, fastened between a bottom and top rail.

Base or Baseboard—A board placed against the wall around a room next to the floor to provide a proper finish between the floor and plaster.

Base Molding—Molding used to trim the upper edge of interior baseboard.

Base Shoe—Molding used next to the floor on interior baseboard. Sometimes called a carpet strip.

Batten—Narrow strips of wood or metal used to cover joints.

Batter Board—One of a pair of horizontal boards nailed to posts set at the corners of an excavation, used to indicate the desired level. Also a fastening for stretched strings to indicate the outlines of foundation walls.

Bay Window—Any window space projecting outward from the walls of a building, either square or polygonal in plan.

Beam—A structural member transversely supporting a load.

Bearing Partition—A partition that supports any vertical load in addition to its own weight.

Bearing Wall—A wall that supports any vertical load in addition to its own weight.

Bed Molding—A molding set in an angle, as between an overhanging cornice or eaves, of a building and the side walls.

Blinds (Shutters)—Light wood sections in the form of doors to close over windows to shut out light, give protection, or add temporary insulation. Commonly used for ornamental purposes, in which case they are fastened rigidly to the building.

Blind-Nailing—Nailing in such a way that the nailheads are not visible on the face of the work.

Blind Stop—A rectangular molding, usually $3/4$ by $1^3/8$ inches or more, used in the assembly of a window frame.

Blue Stain—A bluish or grayish discoloration of the sapwood caused by the growth of certain moldlike fungi on the surface and in the interior of the piece, made possible by the same conditions that favor the growth of other fungi.

Bolster—A short horizontal timber resting on the top of a column for the support of beams or girders.

Boston Ridge—A method of applying asphalt or wood shingles as a finish at the ridge or hips of a roof.

Brace—An inclined piece of framing lumber used to complete a triangle, and thereby to stiffen a structure.

Brick Veneer—A facing of brick laid against frame or tile wall construction.

Bridging—Small wood or metal members that are installed in a diagonal position between the floor joists to act both as tension and compression members for the purpose of bracing the joists and spreading the action of loads.

Buck—Often used in reference to rough frame opening members. Door bucks used in reference to metal door frame.

Built-Up Roof—A roofing composed of three to five layers of rag felt or jute saturated with coal tar, pitch, or asphalt. The top is finished with crushed slag or gravel. Generally used on flat or low-pitched roofs.

Butt Joint—The junction where the ends of two timbers or other members meet in a square-cut joint.

Cabinet—A shop- or job-built unit for kitchens. Cabinets often include combinations of drawers, doors, and the like.

Cant Strip—A wedge or triangular-shaped piece of lumber used at the gable ends under the shingles or at the junction of the house and a flat deck under the roofing.

Cap—The upper member of a column, pilaster, door cornice, molding, and the like.

Casement Frames and Sash—Frames of wood or metal enclosing part or all of the sash, which may be opened by means of hinges affixed to the vertical edges.

Casing—Wide molding of various widths and thicknesses used to trim door and window openings.

Checking—Cracks that appear with age in many exterior paint coatings, at first superficial, but which in time may penetrate entirely through the coating.

Checkrails—Meeting rails sufficiently thicker than a window to fill the opening between the top and bottom sash made by the parting stop in the frame. They are usually beveled.

Collar Beam—A beam connecting pairs of opposite rafters above the attic floor.

Column—In architecture: A perpendicular supporting member, circular or rectangular in section, usually consisting of a base, shaft, and capital. In engineering: A structural compression member, usually vertical, supporting loads acting on or near and in the direction of its longitudinal axis.

Concrete, Plain—Concrete without reinforcement, or reinforced only for shrinkage or temperature changes.

Condensation—Beads or drops of water, and frequently frost in extremely cold weather, that accumulate on the inside of the exterior covering of a building when warm, moisture-laden air from the interior reaches a point where the temperature no longer permits the air to sustain the moisture it holds. Use of louvers or attic ventilators will reduce moisture condensation in attics.

Conduit, Electrical—A pipe, usually metal, in which wire is installed.

Construction, Drywall—A type of construction in which the interior wall finish is applied in a dry condition, generally in the form of sheet materials, as contrasted to plaster.

Construction, Frame—A type of construction in which the structural parts are of wood or dependent upon a wood frame for support. In codes, if brick or other incombustible material is applied to the exterior walls, the classification of this type of construction is usually unchanged.

Coped Joint—See *Scribing*.

Corbel Out—To build out one or more courses of brick or stone from the face of a wall, to form a support for timbers.

Corner Bead—A strip of galvanized iron, sometimes combined with a strip of metal lath, which is placed on corners before plastering to reinforce them. Also, a strip of wood finish three-quarters round or angular placed over a plastered corner for protection.

Corner Boards—Used as trim for the external corners of a house or other frame structure against which the ends of the siding are finished.

Corner Braces—Diagonal braces let into studs to reinforce corners of frame structures.

Cornerite—Metal-mesh lath cut into strips and bent to a right angle. Used in interior corners of walls and ceilings on lath to prevent cracks in plastering.

Cornice—A decorative element made up of molded members usually placed at or near the top of an exterior or interior wall.

Cornice Return—That portion of the cornice that returns on the gable end of a house.

Counterflashing—A flashing usually used on chimneys at the roofline to cover shingle flashing and to prevent moisture entry.

Cove Molding—A three-sided molding with concave face used wherever small angles are to be covered.

Crawl Space—A shallow space below the living quarters of a house. It is generally not excavated or paved and is often enclosed for appearance by a skirting or facing material.

Cricket—A small drainage diverting roof structure of single or double slope placed at the junction of larger surfaces that meet at an angle.

Crown Molding—A molding used on a cornice or wherever a large angle is to be covered.

d—See *Penny*.

Dado—A rectangular groove in a board or plank. In interior decoration, a special type of wall treatment.

Decay—Disintegration of wood or other substance through the action of fungi.

Deck paint—An enamel with a high degree of resistance to mechanical wear, for use on such surfaces as porch floors.

Density—The mass of substance in a unit volume. When expressed in the metric system, it is numerically equal to the specific gravity of the same substance.

Dimension—See *Lumber, Dimension*.

Direct Nailing—To nail perpendicular to the initial surface or to the junction of the pieces joined. Also termed *face nailing*.

Doorjamb, Interior—The surrounding case into which and out of which a door closes and opens. It consists of two upright pieces, called jambs, and a head, fitted together and rabbeted.

Dormer—An internal recess, the framing of which projects from a sloping roof.

Downspout—A pipe, usually of metal, for carrying rain water from roof gutters.

Dressed and Matched (Tongue and Groove)—Boards or planks machined in such a manner that there is a groove on one edge and a corresponding tongue on the other.

Drier, Paint—Usually oil-soluble soaps of such metals as lead, manganese, or cobalt, which, in small proportions, hasten the oxidation and hardening (drying) of the drying oils in paints.

Drip—(*a*) A member of a cornice or other horizontal exterior-finish course that has a projection beyond the other parts for throwing off water. (*b*) A groove in the under side of a sill to cause water to drop off on the outer edge, instead of drawing back and running down the face of the building.

Drip Cap—A molding placed on the exterior top side of a door or window to cause water to drip beyond the outside of the frame.

Ducts—In a house, usually round or rectangular metal pipes for distributing warm air from the heating plant to rooms, or air from a conditioning device. Ducts are also made of asbestos and composition materials.

Eaves—The margin or lower part of a roof projecting over the wall.

Expansion Joint—A bituminous fiber strip used to separate blocks or units of concrete to prevent cracking due to expansion as a result of temperature changes.

Facia or Fascia—A flat board, band, or face, used sometimes by itself but usually in combination with moldings, located at the outer face of the cornice.

Filler (Wood)—A heavily pigmented preparation used for filling and leveling off the pores in open-pored woods.

Fire-Resistive—In the absence of a specific ruling by the authority having jurisdiction, applies to materials for construction not combustible in the temperatures of ordinary fires and that will withstand such fires without serious impairment of their usefulness for at least 1 hour.

Fire-Retardant Chemical—A chemical or preparation of chemicals used to reduce flammability or to retard spread of flame.

Fire Stop—A solid, tight closure of a concealed space, placed to prevent the spread of fire and smoke through such a space.

Flagstone (Flagging or Flags)—Flat stones, from 1 to 4 inches thick, used for rustic walks, steps, floors, and the like. Usually sold by the ton.

Flashing—Sheet metal or other material used in roof and wall construction to protect a building from seepage of water.

Flat Paint—An interior paint that contains a high proportion of pigment and dries to a flat or lusterless finish.

Flue—The space or passage in a chimney through which smoke, gas, or fumes ascend. Each passage is called a flue, which, together with any others and the surrounding masonry, makes up the chimney.

Flue Lining—Fire clay or terra-cotta pipe, round or square, usually made in all of the ordinary flue sizes and in 2-foot lengths, used for the inner lining of chimneys with the brick or masonry work around the outside. Flue lining should run from the concrete footing to the top of the chimney cap. Figure a foot of flue lining for each foot of chimney.

Footing—The spreading course or courses at the base or bottom of a foundation wall, pier, or column.

Foundation—The supporting portion of a structure below the first-floor construction, or below grade, including the footings.

Framing, Balloon—A system of framing a building in which all vertical structural elements of the bearing walls and partitions consist of single pieces extending from the top of the soleplate to the roofplate and to which all floor joists are fastened.

Framing, Platform—A system of framing a building in which floor joists of each story rest on the top plates of the story below or on the foundation sill for the first story, and the bearing walls and partitions rest on the subfloor of each story.

Frieze—Any sculptured or ornamental band in a building. Also the horizontal member of a cornice set vertically against the wall.

Frostline—The depth of frost penetration in soil. This depth varies in different parts of the country. Footings should be placed below this depth to prevent movement.

Fungi, Wood—Microscopic plants that live in damp wood and cause mold, stain, and decay.

Fungicide—A chemical that is poisonous to fungi.

Furring—Strips of wood or metal applied to a wall or other surface to even it, to form an air space, or to give the wall an appearance of greater thickness.

Gable—That portion of a wall contained between the slope of a single-sloped roof and a line projected horizontally through the lowest elevation of the roof construction.

Gable End—An end wall having a gable.

Gloss (Paint or Enamel)—A paint that contains a relatively low proportion of pigment and dries to a sheen or luster.

Gloss Enamel—A finishing material made of varnish and sufficient pigments to provide opacity and color, but little or no pigment of low opacity. Such an enamel forms a hard coating that has a maximum smoothness of surface and a high degree of gloss.

Girder—A large or principal beam used to support concentrated loads at isolated points along its length.

Grain—The direction, size, arrangement, appearance, or quality of the fibers in wood.

Grain, Edge (Vertical)—Edge-grain lumber has been sawed parallel to the pith of the log and approximately at right angles to the growth rings; i.e., the rings form an angle of 45° or more with the surface of the piece.

Grain, Flat—Flat-grain lumber has been sawed parallel to the pith of the log and approximately at right angles to the growth rings; i.e., the rings form an angle of less than 45° with the surface of the piece.

Grain, Quartersawn—Another term for edge grain.

Grounds—Strips of wood, of the same thickness as the lath and plaster, that are attached to walls before the plastering is done. Used around windows, doors, and other openings as a plaster stop and in other places for the purpose of attaching baseboards or other trim.

Grout—Mortar made of such consistency by the addition of water that it will just flow into the joints and cavities of the masonry work and fill them solid.

Gutter—A shallow channel or conduit of metal, wood, or plastic set below and along the eaves of a house to catch and carry off rain water from the roof.

Gypsum Plaster—Gypsum formulated to be used with the addition of sand and water for base-coat plaster.

Header—*(a)* A beam placed perpendicular to joists and to which joists are nailed in framing for chimney, stairway, or other opening. *(b)* A wood lintel.

Hearth—The floor of a fireplace, usually made of brick, tile, or stone.

Heartwood—The wood extending from the pith to the sapwood, the cells of which no longer participate in the life processes of the tree.

Hip—The external angle formed by the meeting of two sloping sides of a roof.

Hip Roof—A roof that rises by inclined planes from all four sides of a building.

Humidifier—A device designed to discharge water vapor into a confined space for the purpose of increasing or maintaining the relative humidity in an enclosure.

I-Beam—A steel beam with a cross section resembling the letter "I."

Insulation, Building—Any material high in resistance to heat transmission that, when placed in the walls, ceilings, or floor of a structure, will reduce the rate of heat flow.

Jack Rafter—A rafter that spans the distance from the wallplate to a hip, or from a valley to a ridge.

Jamb—The side post or lining of a doorway, window, or other opening.

Joint—The space between the adjacent surfaces of two members or components joined and held together by nails, glue, cement, mortar, or other means.

Joint Cement—A powder that is usually mixed with water and used for joint treatment in gypsum-wallboard finish. Often called *spackle*.

Joist—One of a series of parallel beams used to support floor and ceiling loads, and supported in turn by larger beams, girders, or bearing walls.

Knot—That portion of a branch or limb that has become incorporated in the body of a tree.

Landing—A platform between flights of stairs or at the termination of a flight of stairs.

Lath—A building material of wood, metal, gypsum or insulating board that is fastened to the frame of a building to act as a plaster base.

Lattice—An assemblage of wood or metal strips, rods, or bars made by crossing them to form a network.

Leader—See *Downspout*.

Ledger Strip—A strip of lumber nailed along the bottom of the side of a girder on which joists rest.

Light—Space in a window sash for a single pane of glass. Also, a pane of glass.

Lintel—A horizontal structural member that supports the load over an opening such as a door or window.

Lookout—A short wood bracket or cantilever to support an overhanging portion of a roof or the like, usually concealed from view.

Louver—An opening with a series of horizontal slats so arranged as to permit ventilation but to exclude rain, sunlight, or vision. See also *Attic Ventilators*.

Lumber—Lumber is the product of the sawmill and planing mill not further manufactured other than by sawing, resawing, and passing lengthwise through a standard planing machine, crosscut to length, and matched.

Lumber, Boards—Yard lumber less than 2 inches thick and 2 or more inches wide.

Lumber, Dimension—Yard lumber from 2 inches to, but not including, 5 inches thick, and 2 or more inches wide. Includes joists, rafters, studding, planks, and small timbers.

Lumber, Dressed Size—The dimensions of lumber after shrinking from the green dimension and after planing, usually $1/2$ inch less than the nominal or rough size. For example, a 2-by-4 stud actually measures $1^1/2$ by $3^1/2$ inches.

Lumber, Matched—Lumber that is edge-dressed and shaped to make a close tongue-and-groove joint at the edges or ends when laid edge to edge or end to end.

Lumber, Shiplap—Lumber that is edge-dressed to make a close rabbeted or lapped joint.

Lumber, Timbers—Lumber 5 or more inches in the least dimension. Includes beams, stringers, posts, caps, sills, girders, and purlins.

Mantel—The shelf above a fireplace. Originally referred to the beam or lintel supporting the arch above the fireplace opening. Used also in referring to the entire finish around a fireplace, covering the chimney breast across the front and sometimes on the sides.

Masonry—Stone, brick, concrete, hollow tile, concrete block, gypsum block, or other similar building units or materials or a combination of the same, bonded together with mortar to form a wall, pier, buttress, or similar mass.

Metal Lath—Sheets of metal that are slit and drawn out to form openings on which plaster is spread.

Millwork—Generally all building materials made of finished wood and manufactured in millwork plants and planing mills are included under the term *millwork*. It includes such items as inside and outside doors, window and doorframes, blinds, porchwork, mantels, panelwork, stairways, moldings, and interior trim. It does not include flooring, ceiling, or siding.

Miter—The joining of two pieces at an angle that bisects the angle of junction.

Moisture Content of Wood—Weight of the water contained in the wood, usually expressed as a percentage of the weight of the oven-dry wood.

Mortise—A slot cut into a board, plank, or timber, usually edgewise, to receive the tenon of another board, plank, or timber to form a joint.

Molding—Material, usually patterned strips, used to provide ornamental variation of outline or contour, whether projections or cavities, such as cornices, bases, window and doorjambs, and heads.

Mullion—A slender bar or pier forming a division between panels or units of windows, screens, or similar frames.

Muntin—The members dividing the glass or openings of sash, doors, and the like.

Natural Finish—A transparent finish, usually a drying oil, sealer, or varnish, applied on wood for the purpose of protection against soiling or weathering. Such a finish may not seriously alter the original color of the wood or obscure its grain pattern.

Newel—Any post to which a stair railing or balustrade is fastened.

Nonbearing Wall—A wall supporting no load other than its own weight.

Nosing—The projecting edge of a molding or drip. Usually applied to the projecting molding on the edge of a stair tread.

O. C. (On Center)—The measurement of spacing for studs, rafters, joists, and the like in a building from the center of one member to the center of the next member.

O. G. (Ogee)—A molding with a profile in the form of a letter S; having the outline of a reversed curve.

Paint—L, pure white lead (basic-carbonate) paint; TLZ, titanium-lead-zinc paint; TZ, titanium-zinc paint.

Panel—A large, thin board or sheet of lumber, plywood, or other material. A thin board with all its edges inserted in a groove of a surrounding frame of thick material. A portion of a flat surface recessed or sunk below the surrounding area, distinctly set off by molding or some other decorative device. Also, a section of floor, wall, ceiling, or roof, usually prefabricated and of large size, handled as a single unit in the operations of assembly and erection.

Paper, Building—A general term for papers, felts, and similar sheet materials used in buildings without reference to their properties or uses.

Paper, Sheathing—A building material, generally paper or felt, used in wall and roof construction as a protection against the passage of air and sometimes moisture.

Parting Stop or Strip—A small wood piece used in the side and head jambs of double-hung windows to separate the upper and lower sash.

Partition—A wall that subdivides spaces within any story of a building.

Penny—As applied to nails, it originally indicated the price per hundred. The term now serves as a measure of nail length and is abbreviated by the letter *d*.

Pier—A column of masonry, usually rectangular in horizontal cross section, used to support other structural members.

Pigment—A powdered solid in suitable degree of subdivision for use in paint or enamel.

Pitch—The incline or rise of a roof. Pitch is expressed in inches or rise per foot of run, or by the ratio of the rise to the span.

Pitch Pocket—An opening extending parallel to the annual rings of growth, that usually contains, or has contained, either solid or liquid pitch.

Pith—The small, soft core at the original center of a tree around which wood formation takes place.

Plate—*(a)* A horizontal structural member placed on a wall or supported on posts, studs, or corbels to carry the trusses of a roof or to carry the rafters directly. *(b)* A shoe, or base member, as of a partition or other frame. *(c)* A small, relatively flat member placed on or in a wall to support girders, rafters, etc.

Plough—To cut a groove, as in a plank.

Plumb—Exactly perpendicular; vertical.

Ply—A term to denote the number of thicknesses or layers of roofing felt, veneer in plywood, or layers in built-up materials, in any finished piece of such material.

Plywood—A piece of wood made of three or more layers of veneer joined with glue and usually laid with the grain of adjoining plies at right angles. Almost always an odd number of plies are used to provide balanced construction.

Porch—A floor extending beyond the exterior walls of a building. It may be covered and enclosed or unenclosed.

Pores—Wood cells of comparatively large diameter that have open ends and are set one above the other to form continuous tubes. The openings of the vessels on the surface of a piece of wood are referred to as pores.

Preservative—Any substance that, for a reasonable length of time, will prevent the action of wood-destroying fungi, borers of various kinds, and similar destructive life when the wood has been properly coated or impregnated with it.

Primer—The first coat of paint in a paint job that consists of two or more coats; also the paint used for such a first coat.

Putty—A type of cement usually made of whiting and boiled linseed oil, beaten or kneaded to the consistency of dough and formerly used in sealing glass in sash. Today glazing compound is used instead.

Quarter Round—A molding that presents a profile of a quarter circle.

Rabbet—A rectangular longitudinal groove cut in the corner of a board or other piece of material.

Radiant Heating—A method of heating, usually consisting of coils or pipes placed in the floor, wall, or ceiling.

Rafter—One of a series of structural members of a roof designed to support roof loads. The rafters of a flat roof are sometimes called roof joists.

Rafter, Hip—A rafter that forms the intersection of an external roof angle.

Rafter, Jack—A rafter that spans the distance from a wallplate to a hip or from a valley to a ridge.

Rafter, Valley—A rafter that forms the intersection of an internal roof angle.

Rail—A horizontal bar or timber of wood or metal extending from one post or support to another as a guard or barrier in a fence, balustrade, staircase, etc. Also, the cross or horizontal members of the framework of a sash, door, blind, or any paneled assembly.

Rake—The trim members that run parallel to the roof slope and from the finish between wall and roof.

Raw Linseed Oil—The crude product expressed from flaxseed and usually without much subsequent treatment.

Reinforcing—Steel rods or metal fabric placed in concrete slabs, beams, or columns to increase their strength.

Relative Humidity—The amount of water vapor expressed as a percentage of the maximum quantity that could be present in the atmosphere at a given temperature. (The actual amount of water vapor that can be held in space increases with the temperature.)

Resin-Emulsion Paint—Paint, the vehicle (liquid part) of which consists of resin or varnish dispersed in fine droplets in water, analogous to cream (which is butterfat dispersed in water).

Ribbon—A narrow board let into the studding to add support to joists.

Ridge—The horizontal line at the junction of the top edges of two sloping roof surfaces. The rafters are nailed at the ridge.

Ridge Board—The board placed on edge at the ridge of the roof to support the upper ends of the rafters.

Rise—The height a roof rising in horizontal distance (run) from the outside face of a wall supporting the rafters or trusses to the ridge of the roof. In stairs, the perpendicular height of a step or flight of steps.

Riser—Each of the vertical boards closing the spaces between the treads of the stairways.

Roll Roofing—Roofing material, composed of fiber and saturated with asphalt, that is supplied in rolls containing 108 square feet in 36-inch widths. It is generally furnished in weights of 55 to 90 pounds per roll.

Roof Sheathing—The boards or sheet material fastened to the roof rafters on which the shingles or other roof covering is laid.

Rubber-Emulsion Paint—Paint, the vehicle of which consists of rubber or synthetic rubber dispersed in fine droplets in water.

Run—In reference to roofs, the horizontal distance from the face of a wall to the ridge of the roof. Referring to stairways, the net width of a step; also the horizontal distance covered by a flight of steps.

Sapwood—The outer zone of wood, next to the bark. In the living tree it contains some living cells (the heartwood contains none), as well as dead and dying cells. In most species, it is lighter colored than the heartwood. In all species, it is lacking in decay resistance.

Sash—A single frame containing one or more panes of glass.

Sash Balance—A device, usually operated with a spring, designed to counterbalance window sash. Use of sash balances eliminates the need for sash weights, pulleys, and sash cord.

Saturated Felt—A felt impregnated with tar or asphalt.

Scratch Coat—The first coat of plaster, which is scratched to form a bond for the second coat.

Scribing—Fitting woodwork to an irregular surface.

Sealer—A finishing material, either clear or pigmented, that is usually applied directly over uncoated wood for the purpose of sealing the surface.

Seasoning—Removing moisture from green wood in order to improve its serviceability.

Semigloss Paint or Enamel—A paint or enamel made with a slight insufficiency of nonvolatile vehicle so that its coating, when dry, has some luster but is not highly glossy.

Shake—A handsplit shingle, usually edge grained.

Sheathing—The structural covering, usually wood boards, plywood, or wallboards, placed over exterior studding or rafters of a structure.

Sheathing Paper—See *Paper, Sheathing.*

Shellac—A transparent coating made by dissolving lac, a resinous secretion of the lac bug (a scale insect that thrives in tropical countries, especially India), in alcohol.

Shingles—Roof covering of asphalt, asbestos, wood, tile, slate, or other material cut to stock lengths, widths, and thicknesses.

Shingles, Siding—Various kinds of shingles, some especially designed, that can be used as the exterior side-wall covering for a structure.

Shiplap—See *Lumber, Shiplap*.

Siding—The finish covering of the outside wall of a frame building, whether made of weatherboards, vertical boards with battens, shingles, or other material.

Siding, Bevel (Lap Siding)—Used as the finish siding on the exterior of a house or other structure. It is usually manufactured by resawing dry square-surfaced boards diagonally to produce two wedge-shaped pieces. These pieces commonly run from $3/16$ inch thick on the thin edge to ½ to ¾ inch thick on the other edge, depending on the width of the siding.

Siding, Drop—Usually ¾ inch thick and 6 inches wide, machined into various patterns. Drop siding has tongue-and-groove joints, is heavier, has more structural strength, and is frequently used on buildings that require no sheathing, such as garages and barns.

Sill—The lowest member of the frame of a structure, resting on the foundation and supporting the uprights of the frame. The member forming the lower side of an opening, as a door sill, window sill, etc.

Soffit—The underside of the members of a building, such as staircases, cornices, beams, and arches, relatively minor in area as compared with ceilings.

Soil Cover (Ground Cover)—A light roll roofing or plastic used on the ground of crawl spaces to minimize moisture permeation of the area.

Soil Stack—A general term for the vertical main of a system of soil, waste, or vent piping.

Sole or Soleplate—A member, usually a 2 by 4, on which wall and partition studs rest.

Span—The distance between structural supports, such as walls, columns, piers, beams, girders, and trusses.

Splash Block—A small masonry block laid with the top close to the ground surface to receive roof drainage and to carry it away from the building.

Square—A unit of measure—100 square feet—usually applied to roofing material. Side-wall coverings are often packed to cover 100 square feet and are sold on that basis.

Stain, Shingle—A form of oil paint, very thin in consistency, intended for coloring wood with rough surfaces, like shingles, but without forming a coating of significant thickness or with any gloss.

Stair Carriage—A stringer for steps on stairs.

Stair Landing—A platform between flights of stairs or at the termination of a flight of stairs.

Stair Rise—The vertical distance from the top of one stair tread to the top of the one next above.

Stool—The flat, narrow shelf forming the top member of the interior trim at the bottom of a window.

Storm Sash or Storm Window—An extra window usually placed on the outside of an existing window as additional protection against cold weather.

Story—That part of a building between floors and the floor or roof above.

String, Stringer—A timber or other support for cross members. In stairs, the support on which the stair treads rest; also *stringboard*.

Stucco—Most commonly refers to an outside plaster made with Portland cement as its base.

Stud—One of a series of slender wood or metal structural members placed as supporting elements in walls and partitions. (Plural: studs or studding.)

Subfloor—Boards or sheet material laid on joists over which a finish floor is to be laid.

Tail Beam—A relatively short beam or joist supported in a wall on one end and by a header on the other.

Termite—Insects that superficially resemble ants in size, general appearance, and habit of living in colonies; hence, they are frequently called *white ants*. Subterranean termites do not establish themselves in buildings by being carried in with lumber but by entering from ground nests after the building has been constructed. If unmolested, they eat out the woodwork, leaving a shell of sound wood to conceal their activities, and damage may proceed so far as to cause collapse of parts of a structure before discovery. There are about 56 species of termites known in the United States; but the two major species, classified from the manner in which they attack wood, are ground-inhabiting or subterranean termites, the most common, and dry-wood termites, found almost exclusively along the extreme southern border and the Gulf of Mexico in the United States.

Termite Shield—A shield, usually of noncorrodible metal, placed in or on a foundation wall or other mass of masonry or around pipes to prevent passage of termites.

Threshold—A strip of wood or metal beveled on each edge and used above the finished floor under outside doors.

Toenailing—To drive a nail at a slant with the initial surface in order to permit it to penetrate into a second member.

Tread—The horizontal board in a stairway on which the foot is placed.

Trim—The finish materials in a building, such as moldings, applied around openings (window trim, door trim) or at the floor and ceiling of rooms (baseboard, cornice, picture molding).

Trimmer—A beam or joist to which a header is nailed in framing for a chimney, stairway, or other opening.

Truss—A frame or jointed structure designed to act as a beam of long span, while each member is usually subjected to longitudinal stress only, either tension or compression.

Turpentine—A volatile oil used as a thinner in paints and as a solvent in varnishes. Chemically, it is a mixture of terpenes.

Undercoat—A coating applied prior to the finishing or top coats of a paint job. It may be the first of two or the second of three coats. In some usage of the word it may become synonymous with priming coat.

Valley—The internal angle formed by the junction of two sloping sides of a roof.

Vapor Barrier—Material used to retard the flow of vapor or moisture into walls and thus to prevent condensation within them. There are two types of vapor barriers, the membrane that comes in rolls and is applied as a unit in the wall or ceiling construction, and the paint type, which is applied with a brush. The vapor barrier must be a part of the warm side of the wall.

Varnish—A thickened preparation of drying oil, or drying oil and resin, suitable for spreading on surfaces to form continuous, transparent coatings, or for mixing with pigments to make enamels.

Vehicle—A liquid portion of a finishing material; it consists of the binder (nonvolatile) and volatile thinners.

Veneer—Thin sheets of wood.

Vent—A pipe installed to provide a flow of air to or from a drainage system or to provide a circulation of air within such systems to protect trap seals from siphonage and back pressure.

Vermiculite—A mineral closely related to mica, with the faculty of expanding on heating to form lightweight material with insulation quality. Used as bulk insulation and also as aggregate in insulating and acoustical plaster and in insulating concrete floors.

Volatile Thinner—A liquid that evaporates readily and is used to thin or reduce the consistency of finishes without altering the relative volumes of pigments and nonvolatile vehicle.

328

Wallboard—Woodpulp, gypsum, or other materials made into large rigid sheets that may be fastened to the frame of a building to provide a surface finish.

Wane—Bark, or lack of wood or bark from any cause, on the edge or corner of a piece.

Wash—The upper surface of a member or material when given a slope to shed water.

Water Repellent—A liquid designed to penetrate into wood and to impart water repellency to the wood.

Water Table—A ledge or offset on or above a foundation wall, for the purpose of shedding water.

Weatherstrip—Narrow strips made of metal, or other material, so designed that when installed at doors or windows they will retard the passage of air, water, moisture, or dust around the door or window sash.

Wood Rays—Strips of cells extending radially within a tree and varying in height from a few cells in some species to 4 inches or more in oak. The rays serve primarily to store food and to transport it horizontally in the tree.

Useful Information

To find the circumference of a circle, multiply the diameter by 3.1416.

To find the diameter of a circle, multiply the circumference by .31831.

To find the area of a circle, multiply the square of the diameter by .7854.

The radius of a circle × 6.283185 = the circumference.

The square of the circumference of a circle × .07958 = the area.

Half the circumference of a circle × half its diameter = the area.

The circumference of a circle × .159155 = the radius.

The square root of the area of a circle × .56419 = the radius.

The square root of the area of a circle × 1.12838 = the diameter.

To find the diameter of a circle equal in area to a given square, multiply a side of the square by 1.12838.

To find the side of a square equal in area to a given circle, multiply the diameter by .8862.

To find the side of a square inscribed in a circle, multiply the diameter of the circle by .7071.

To find the side of a hexagon inscribed in a circle, multiply the diameter of the circle by .500.

To find the diameter of a circle inscribed in a hexagon multiply a side of the hexagon by 1.7321.

To find the side of an equilateral triangle inscribed in a circle multiply the diameter of the circle by .866.

To find the diameter of a circle inscribed in an equilateral triangle, multiply a side of the triangle by .57735.

To find the area of the surface of a ball (sphere), multiply the square of the diameter by 3.1416.

To find the volume of a ball (sphere), multiply the cube of the diameter by .5236.

Doubling the diameter of a pipe increases its capacity four times.

To find the pressure in pounds per square inch at the base of a column of water, multiply the height of the column in feet by .433.

A gallon of water (U.S. Standard) weighs 8.336 pounds and contains 231 cubic inches. A cubic foot of water contains 7½ gallons, 1728 cubic inches, and weighs 62.425 pounds at a temperature of about 39° F.

Index